INDIANA
SCIENCE
Fusion

fusion [FYOO • zhuhn] a mixture or blend formed by fusing two or more things

This Interactive Student Edition belongs to

_____

Teacher/Room

_____

 HOUGHTON MIFFLIN HARCOURT

HOUGHTON MIFFLIN HARCOURT

Front Cover: *stingray* ©Jeffrey L. Rotman/Corbis; *moth* ©Millard H. Sharp/Photo Researchers, Inc.; *astronaut* ©NASA; *thermometer* ©StockImages/Alamy; *robotic arm* ©Garry Gay/The Image Bank/Getty Images.

Back Cover: *rowers* ©Stockbyte/Getty Images; *beaker* ©Gregor Schuster/Getty Images; *tree frog* ©DLILLC/Corbis; *Great Basin National Park* ©Frans Lanting/Corbis.

ISBN   978-0-547-43843-6

5 6 7 8 9 10   0877   19 18 17 16 15 14 13 12
4500360518   BCDEFG

Consulting Authors

Michael A. DiSpezio
Global Educator
North Falmouth, Massachusetts

Marjorie Frank
Science Writer and Content-Area Reading Specialist
Brooklyn, New York

Michael Heithaus
Director, School of Environment and Society
Associate Professor, Department of Biological Sciences
Florida International University
North Miami, Florida

Donna Ogle
Professor of Reading and Language
National-Louis University
Chicago, Illinois

Program Advisors

Paul D. Asimow
Professor of Geology and Geochemistry
California Institute of Technology
Pasadena, California

Bobby Jeanpierre
Associate Professor of Science Education
University of Central Florida
Orlando, Florida

Gerald H. Krockover
Professor of Earth and Atmospheric Science Education
Purdue University
West Lafayette, Indiana

Rose Pringle
Associate Professor School of Teaching and Learning
College of Education
University of Florida
Gainesville, Florida

Carolyn Staudt
Curriculum Designer for Technology
KidSolve, Inc.
The Concord Consortium
Concord, Massachusetts

Larry Stookey
Science Department
Antigo High School
Antigo, Wisconsin

Carol J. Valenta
Senior Vice President and Associate Director of the Museum
Saint Louis Science Center
St. Louis, Missouri

Barry A. Van Deman
President and CEO
Museum of Life and Science
Durham, North Carolina

Power Up with Science Fusion!

Your program fuses . . .

Online Virtual Experiences

Hands-on Explorations

Active Reading

. . . to generate new science energy for today's science learner—*you.*

Active Reading

Be an active reader and make this book your own!

You can write your ideas, answer questions, draw graphs, make notes, and record your activity results right on these pages.

By the end of the school year, this book becomes a record of everything you learn in science.

escribe

n use all the words you see h
You can use your senses to find
color, taste, size, shape, odor, or te

tive ing As you read these two pages, circle words
hrases t al a detail about physical properties.

ardness
hard. The grapes
cribes how easily
d or dent.

Co
e words we use for describe
way light bounces object.
at colors do you see

Taste
ckers are salty. Candy can taste
t or sour. Can you think of
so hing that tastes bitter?

Textu
feels l
textur

These s
has a ni
you if m

Hands-on Explorations

Science is all about doing.

There are lots of exciting investigations on the Inquiry Flipchart.

Ask questions and test your ideas.

Draw conclusions and share what you learn.

How Can You Model a School?

There are many types of models: mental models, two-dimensional, three-dimensional, and computer models. In this activity, you'll model a part of your school.

1. With a team, choose a part of your school to model. It may be a single room, a floor, or a whole building.

2. Next, choose two types of models to make. Get permission from your teacher to carry out your plans.

3. With your team, choose the materials you will use. Make any measurements you need, and record them carefully.

4. Make the two models, and compare them to those of other teams.

Online Virtual Experiences

Explore cool labs and activities in the virtual world—where science comes alive and you make it happen.

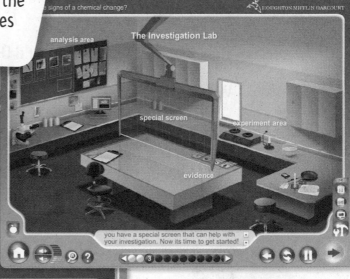

See your science lessons from a completely different point of view—a digital point of view.

Science Fusion is new energy... just for YOU!

Contents

PROCESS STANDARDS
Nature of Science

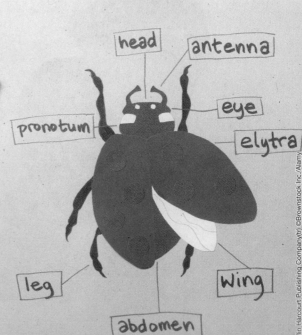

head antenna eye elytra pronotum leg wing abdomen

STANDARD 1
Physical Science

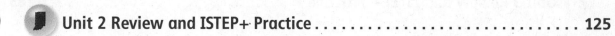

STANDARD 3
Life Science

STANDARD 4
Science, Engineering
and Technology

Unit 5—Forces and Transportation 241

PROCESS STANDARDS
Nature of Science

Crinoid fossil

I Wonder Why

Why is this scientist using a wooden brush to clean a rock? *Turn the page to find out.*

Here's Why Ancient fossils, like the crinoid and the duck-billed dinosaur jawbone, can be very delicate. Scientists must use the right tools to uncover the fossil without damaging it.

Track Your Progress

Essential Questions and Indiana Standards

PROCESS STANDARDS
Nature of Science

Students gain scientific knowledge by observing the natural and constructed world, performing and evaluating investigations and communicating their findings. These principles should guide student work and be integrated into the curriculum along with the content standards on a daily basis.

The Nature of Science Students gain scientific knowledge by observing the natural and constructed world, performing and evaluating investigations and communicating their findings. These principles should guide student work and be integrated into the curriculum along with the content standards on a daily basis.

Lesson **1**

Essential Question

What Do Scientists Do?

Engage Your Brain!

Find the answer to the following question in this lesson and record it here.

Biologists make observations about living things. What are some observations you can make about lizards?

_____

_____

_____

_____

Active Reading

Lesson Vocabulary

List the terms. As you learn about each one, make notes in the Interactive Glossary.

_____   _____

_____   _____

_____   _____

Main Ideas

In this lesson, you'll read about how scientists do their work. Active readers look for main ideas before they read to give their reading a purpose. Often, the headings in a lesson state its main ideas. Preview the headings in this lesson to give your reading a purpose.

The Role of Scientists

It's career day for Mr. Green's fourth-grade class! Mr. Green invited a scientist named Dr. Sims to talk to the class. The students are ready, and they have many questions to ask.

Active Reading As you read these two pages, turn the heading into a question in your mind. Then underline the sentence that answers the question.

What do scientists do?

▶ Write a question you would ask a scientist.

_____

_____

_____

_____

"Thank you for inviting me to your school! My name is Dr. Sims, and I am a scientist. A **scientist** asks questions about the natural world. There are many kinds of scientists and many questions to ask!

Science is the study of the natural world. Earth scientists study things like rocks, weather, and the planets. Physical scientists study matter and energy. Life scientists, like me, study living things. I am a wildlife biologist, which means I study animals in the wild.

Scientists work alone and in teams. Sometimes, I travel alone on long hikes to watch animals. At other times, I ask other biologists to go with me. I share ideas with other scientists every day.

Science is hard work but fun, too. I like being outdoors. Discovering something new is exciting. The best part, for me, is helping animals. The best way to explain what a scientist does is to show you."

▶ For each area of science, write a question a scientist might ask.

Earth Science

_____

_____

_____

Life Science

_____

_____

_____

Physical Science

_____

_____

_____

Do you work all by yourself?

Is it fun to be a scientist?

Making Observations and Asking Questions

Dr. Sims looks around the classroom. She observes everything for a few moments. Then she asks questions about what she sees.

How does that plant produce offspring?

Does the lizard's skin ever change colors?

Does the goldfish spend more time near the top of the tank or the bottom of the tank?

Dr. Sims

▶ Ask your own question about the classroom in the photo.

_____

_____

_____

▶ Name five things you observe in this classroom.

_____

_____

_____

Scientists make observations about the world around them. An **observation** is information collected by using the five senses.

Scientists ask questions about their observations. Notice that Dr. Sims' questions are about the living things in the classroom. That's because she is a wildlife biologist. Your questions might be different if you observed different things than she did.

Dr. Sims asks, "How would you find an answer to my question about the goldfish?" She and the students talk about watching the fish. Someone suggests writing observations in a notebook. Someone else says a stopwatch can help.

Dr. Sims says, "I could do all these things in an investigation." Scientists conduct an **investigation** to answer questions. The steps of an investigation may include asking questions, making observations, reading or talking to experts, drawing conclusions, and sharing what you learn.

Experiments

Dr. Sims seems very excited to talk about investigations. She says, "Describing what you see is one kind of investigation. Other investigations include doing an experiment."

Active Reading As you read these two pages, circle the lesson vocabulary word each time it is used.

A Fair Test

An *experiment* is a fair test. It can show that one thing causes another thing to happen. In each test, you change only one factor, or *variable*. To be fair and accurate, you conduct the experiment multiple times.

To test something else, you must start a new experiment. Being creative and working in teams can help scientists conduct experiments.

Carlos is conducting an experiment. He gives the lizard fruit and crickets to see which will be eaten. The food is the only variable that is changed. Each day, the lizard gets two different types of food at the same time and in the same amounts.

Scientific Methods

Scientific investigations use scientific methods. Scientific methods may include the following activities:

- make observations

- ask a question

- form a hypothesis

- plan and conduct an experiment

- record and analyze results

- draw conclusions

- communicate results

Sometimes, these steps are done in this order. At other times, they're not.

A **hypothesis** is an idea or explanation that can be tested with an investigation. Dr. Sims gives the students an example from their classroom. She says, "I hypothesize that this lizard eats more insects than fruit."

▶ Talk with other students in your class. Then write a hypothesis to explain what makes the lizard in the photo change color.

_____

_____

_____

_____

_____

_____

Other Kinds of Investigations

Dr. Sims smiles. She says, "I hope this doesn't confuse anyone, but doing an experiment isn't always possible."

Active Reading As you read these two pages, circle the clue words or phrases that signal a detail such as an example or an added fact.

Many science questions cannot be answered by doing an experiment. Here's one question: What kind of lizard have I found? This question can be answered by using an identification guide. Here's another question: What causes the sun to seem to rise and set? This question can be answered by making and using a model of Earth and the sun. Here's another: At what time of year does a state get the most rain? This question can be answered by looking for patterns through many years of rainfall records. Here's another: How did people who lived 100 years ago describe Mars? This question can be answered with research. Research includes reading what others have written and asking experts.

What is the surface of Mars like? This question is hard to answer with an experiment. NASA scientists sent robot spacecraft to Mars. Cameras on these spacecraft take pictures of the planet for scientists to observe.

Use an Identification Guide

Draw lines to match the lizard with its description.

Texas Horned Lizard

- Colors: brownish
- Body: wider and flatter than other lizards
- Tail: straight and shorter than the body
- Spines: several short horns on head, spiny scales on sides of body

Common Chameleon

- Colors: green, yellow, gray, or brown
- Eyes: big and bulge out from side of head
- Body: tall and flat, a ridge of scales along the backbone
- Tail: curls for grasping branches

Common Iguana

- Colors: green, gray, brown, blue, lavender, or black
- Spines: along center of back and tail
- Body: Large flap of skin under the chin

Scientists Share Their Results as Evidence

Dr. Sims says, "Tell me something you know." You tell her that it is going to be stormy tomorrow. She says, "*How* do you know?"

Active Reading As you read these two pages, draw two lines under the main idea.

When scientists explain how things work, they must give evidence. *Evidence* is data gathered during an investigation. Evidence might support your hypothesis, or it might not. For example, think about the class with their lizard. The students tell Dr. Sims a hypothesis: Lizards eat more insects than fruit. They carry out an experiment, putting tiny crickets and fruit in the lizard's tank. After two hours, they observe how much food is left, and then repeat the experiment each day for a week.

The students tell Dr. Sims that their lizard ate more crickets than fruit. She says, "What is your evidence?" The students share their recorded results. They report that the lizard ate 13 crickets and no fruit.

Science Notebook

A *conclusion* is an explanation that is based on evidence. Write conclusions for the evidence given below.

Evidence

We used thermometers and found that when the air temperature changed by 5 degrees, a chameleon's skin color changed.

Conclusion

_____

_____

_____

_____

Evidence

We measured the temperature at the same time each morning and afternoon for one month. Each day, the air temperature was higher in the afternoon than in the morning.

Conclusion

_____

_____

_____

_____

_____

Evidence

Paper Airplane Wingspan (cm)	Time in the Air (sec)
5	7
10	12
15	21
20	28

Conclusion

_____

_____

_____

_____

When you're done, use the answer key to check and revise your work.

Fill in the missing words to tell what scientists do.

Summarize

Mr. Brown's fourth-grade class wants a pet in their classroom. Their teacher says they have to think like a (1) _____ to care for animals. The students know that means (2) _____ about the natural world. The class wonders what kinds of animals make good classroom pets. They decide to do an (3) _____ to find out. They go to the library and use books and websites to (4) _____ pets.

The class concludes that guinea pigs are the best pets for their classroom. Mr. Brown asks them what (5) _____ they have to support their conclusion. The students explain that guinea pigs are quiet and gentle. They are also active in the daytime and sleep at night.

Once the guinea pigs are in the classroom, the students watch and listen. They keep a science journal and list all their (6) _____. Then, students ask (7) _____ based on what they observe. One is: What does it mean when the guinea pigs make squeaking sounds? Two students have a (8) _____ : guinea pigs make that noise when they want to be fed.

Mr. Brown suggests that the students record the time when they hear the sound and write down what they are doing at the same time. After a few days, the students see that their guinea pigs make that noise just as the zippered bag that holds the fresh vegetables is opened. So, what do you think the sound means? (9) _____

_____

14

Name _____

Word Play

1 Use the words in the box to complete the puzzle.

Across

5. An explanation based on evidence

7. Scientists do one of these to answer questions

Down

1. An idea or explanation that can be tested with an investigation

2. To share the results of investigations

3. A person who asks questions about the natural world

4. You ask this

6. A kind of investigation that is a fair test

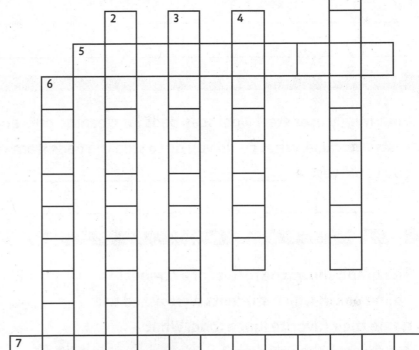

communicate   conclusion   experiment*   hypothesis*

investigation*   question   scientist*

* Key Lesson Vocabulary

Apply Concepts

2 Choose an object to observe. List some observations. Then ask some questions related to your observations.

Name of Object: _____   Questions: _____

Observations: _____   _____

_____   _____

_____   _____

_____   _____

3 Your family uses steel wool soap pads for cleaning pots and pans. Often they get rusty after use. What could you do to stop the pads from rusting? Write a hypothesis you could test. _____

_____

4 The graph shows the results of a national online poll in which students were asked to name their favorite lunch food. What conclusions can you draw? _____

_____

_____

_____

_____

Pita pockets

Grilled cheese

Pizza

Lasagna

Hamburgers

Take It Home!

You can think like a scientist at home, too. Which window cleaner leaves fewer streaks? What kind of bird did I see outside my window? Make a list of questions with your family. Investigate them together.

The **Nature of Science** Students gain scientific knowledge by observing the natural and constructed world, performing and evaluating investigations and communicating their findings. These principles should guide student work and be integrated into the curriculum along with the content standards on a daily basis.

Lesson **2**

Essential Question

What Skills Do Scientists Use?

Engage Your Brain!

Find the answer to the following question in the lesson and record it here.

Splash it. Pour it. Freeze it. Make bubbles in it. What skills might a scientist use to test how water behaves?

_____

_____

_____

_____

Active Reading

Lesson Vocabulary

List the terms. As you learn about each one, make notes in the interactive Glossary.

_____

_____

_____

Visual Aids

In this lesson, you'll see large graphics with labels. The labels call attention to important details. Active readers preview a lesson's graphics and decide how the information in them provides details about the main idea.

Everyday Science Skills

Do you ask questions about the world around you? If so, you use these science skills all day, every day—just like a scientist!

Active Reading As you read the next four pages, circle the names of nine science skills.

As you read about scientists, think
→ **"Hey, I can do this, too!"**

Infer

Scientists *infer* how things work by thinking about their observations. A biologist may infer that the color patterns of fish enable them to blend in and avoid predators.

Observe

Scientists may *observe* many things, such as changes in color, temperature, and bubbling.

Scientists use inquiry skills every day—and so do you. When you observe, you use your five senses to get information. Let's say you smell cheese, bread, and spicy odors. You *infer* "I think we are having pizza for lunch today!" An **inference** is a statement that explains an observation.

When you think about how things are the same and different, you *compare* them. For example, your family wants to adopt a new kitten. You compare different kittens, looking for one that is playful and friendly. When you decide which kitten is the best, you *communicate* that decision to your family. You can communicate by speaking, writing, and by using pictures or models.

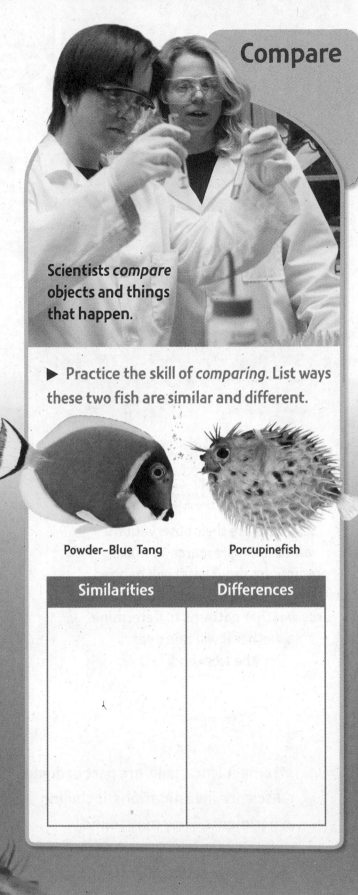

Compare

Scientists *compare* objects and things that happen.

▶ Practice the skill of *comparing*. List ways these two fish are similar and different.

Powder-Blue Tang   Porcupinefish

Similarities	Differences

Communicate

▶ Scientists *communicate,* or share, their results and inferences with other scientists. What did you communicate today?

_____

_____

_____

Think Like a Scientist

Scientists use these skills every day in their investigations. Find out what they are and when you might use them.

Predict

Scientists use their observations and existing research to make predictions about what will happen in the future. For example, a meteorologist uses weather patterns to determine whether it will rain over the weekend.

Use Variables

When scientists plan experiments, they think, "What is the one thing I will change?" That one thing is a variable. Let's say you want to find out how cold a freezer has to be to make fruit pops. The variable that you will change is the temperature inside the freezer.

Some science skills are part of doing science investigations, including experiments. They may sound unfamiliar to you. But when you read about these skills, you might realize that you already use them.

Plan and Conduct Investigations

Scientists plan and conduct investigations that will answer science questions. Say you want to know how salty water must be to make an egg float. First, you think about the steps you'll take to find the answer. Next, you gather the materials you'll use. Then, you test the amount of salt.

▶ You are a marine biologist. You study living things in the ocean. What is one investigation you might plan?

_____

_____

_____

Predict what a marine biologist might look for on a dive.

_____

_____

_____

Hypothesize

Scientists hypothesize when they think of a testable statement that tries to explain an observation. Suppose you notice that water seems to evaporate at different rates from containers with different shapes. What would you hypothesize is a cause?

Draw Conclusions

Scientists draw conclusions when they use evidence to evaluate a hypothesis. If you investigate how the size of a sail affects how quickly a toy boat moves, you might conclude that boats with larger sails move faster because larger sails collect more wind.

Math and Science Skills

Using rulers and balances. Putting things in order. Measuring the speed of a car. Making tables and graphs. Sounds like math, but it's science, too!

Active Reading As you read this page, turn the heading into a question in your mind. Then underline the parts of the text that answer the question.

Every scientist uses math. Let's say you are a marine biologist who studies whales. You *classify* whales by how much they weigh or how long they are from head to tail. You put them in *order* when you arrange them by length from smallest to largest. You *use numbers* to tell how many are alive today. You *use time and space relationships* to investigate when and where they migrate each year. You *measure* how long they are and how much food they eat. You *record and display* the results of your investigations in writing and in tables, graphs, and maps.

Classify and Order

You classify things when you put them into groups. To put things in order, you may make a list in which position matters, such as ordering bird species by how fast they fly or move.

Measure

In science and math, you measure by using tools to find length, width, height, mass, weight, volume, and elapsed time.

Use Numbers

You use numbers when you observe by counting or measuring. You also use numbers to compare and order. And, you use numbers to describe speed and force.

Do the Math!
Compare Numbers

Some of the world's biggest mammals live under the oceans' waves. The table gives the names of several kinds of whales and the number that scientists estimate are alive today.

Kind of Whale	Population
Beluga whale	200,000
Blue whale	14,000
Fin whale	55,000
Humpback whale	40,000
Minke whale	1,000,000
Pilot whale	1,200,000
Sei whale	54,000
Sperm whale	

1. Which two kinds of whales have the closest number alive?

_____

2. How many more Pilot whales are there than Minke whales?

_____

3. Scientists estimate there are about three hundred and sixty thousand sperm whales alive today. Write that number, using numerals, in the table.

Use Time and Space Relationships

You use stopwatches and clocks to tell the time. You can predict when it will be high tide or low tide. You can also determine how the planets move in space.

Record and Display Data

You record observations on clipboards, in notebooks, and on computers. You display, or show, data so that it's easy to understand by making tables, graphs, or diagrams.

Sum It Up!

When you're done, use the answer key to check and revise your work.

Fill in the missing skills in the column where they belong.

Summarize

Scientists Use Skills

Everyday Science Skills	Science Investigation Skills	Math and Science Skills
1. _____	5. _____	10. _____
2. _____	6. _____	11. _____
3. _____	7. _____	12. _____
4. _____	8. _____	13. _____
	9. _____	14. _____

Answer Key: 1–4. infer, communicate, compare, observe; **5–9.** predict, use variables, plan and conduct investigations, draw conclusions, hypothesize; **10–14.** measure, classify and order, record and display data, use time and space relationships, use numbers

Name _____

Word Play

1 It's easy to get tongue-tied describing what scientists do. Look at the statements below. Switch the red words around until each statement about inquiry skills makes sense.

In order to sort his beakers and other tools, Dr. Mallory hypothesizes each object by size and shape. _____

Gabriella measures that her dog will want his favorite food for dinner, because she has observed him eat it quickly many times before. _____

Kim predicts when planning an experiment with her older brother. She keeps everything the same during their procedure, except for the one factor being tested. _____

After completing an experiment and summarizing her findings, Dr. Garcia classifies what she has learned with other scientists. _____

Dr. Jefferson studies the age of rocks and fossils. She uses variables to tell how old each specimen is. _____

Before conducting his experiment for the science fair, Derrick uses time and space relationships about which sample of fertilizer will make his tomato plant grow the fastest. _____

To find out how long it takes Deshawn to ride his bike 100 m, Jessica communicates the time with a stopwatch. _____

Apply Concepts

2 Write how you would use numbers to investigate each object.

_____

_____

_____

_____

_____

_____

_____

_____

_____

_____

_____

_____

3 For each one, what kinds of observations could you record on a calendar?

_____

_____

_____

_____

_____

_____

_____

_____

_____

_____

_____

_____

Take It Home!

There are many books in the library about scientists and how they think about the world around them. Pick a book with a family member. Find examples of the skills you learned about and make a list.

The Nature of Science Students gain scientific knowledge by observing the natural and constructed world, performing and evaluating investigations and communicating their findings. These principles should guide student work and be integrated into the curriculum along with the content standards on a daily basis.

8 Things YOU SHOULD KNOW ABOUT Ayanna Howard

1 Dr. Ayanna Howard is a roboticist. She designs and builds robots.

2 Dr. Howard is making robots that will make decisions without the help of people.

3 To get a robot to make decisions on its own, Dr. Howard must teach the robot how to think.

4 Dr. Howard uses computer programs to teach robots. She observes the robots. Then she changes her computer programs to get better results.

5 Dr. Howard studies how robots can help explore outer space and unsafe places on Earth.

6 Dr. Howard taught a robot called SmartNav to move around things in its path. This robot could explore the surface of Mars.

7 Scientists want to understand why the ice in Antarctica is melting. Dr. Howard's SnoMote robots can safely gather data on the cracking ice sheets.

8 In 2003, Dr. Howard was named a top young inventor.

27

Now You Be a Roboticist!

1 What is Dr. Howard investigating?

2 Why does Dr. Howard test the robots?

3 What scientific question does Dr. Howard's SnoMote help answer?

4 If you were a roboticist, what kind of robot would you make?

5 What steps would you take in making your robot?

6 Draw a picture of your robot.

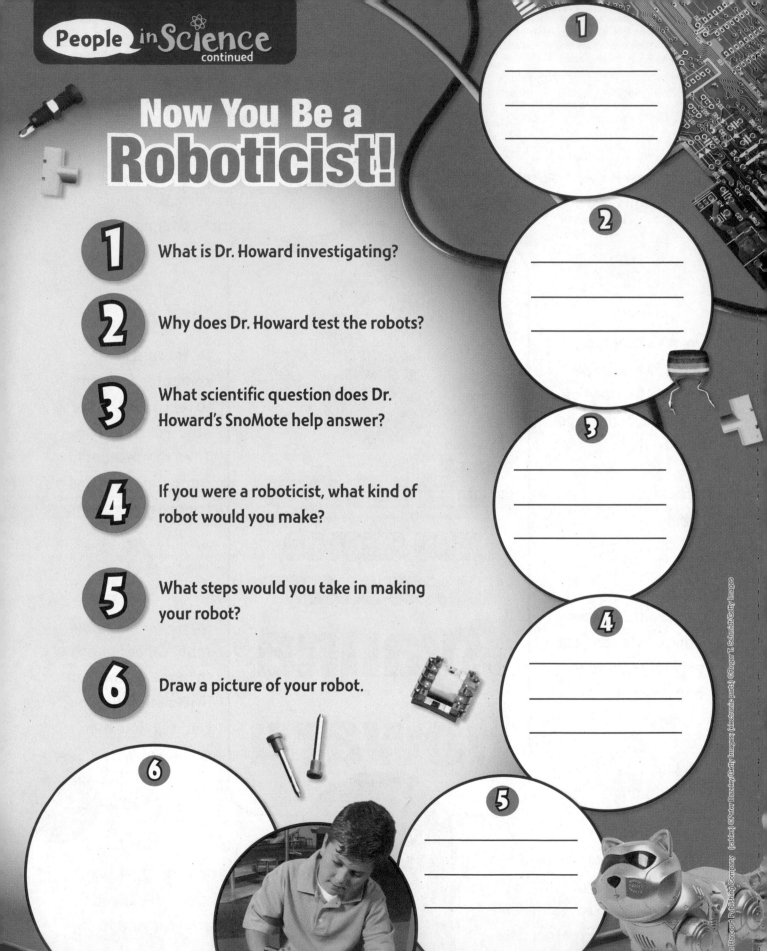

The Nature of Science Students gain scientific knowledge by observing the natural and constructed world, performing and evaluating investigations and communicating their findings. These principles should guide student work and be integrated into the curriculum along with the content standards on a daily basis.

Lesson 3

Essential Question

How Do Scientists Collect and Use Data?

Engage Your Brain!

Find the answer to the following question in this lesson and record it here.

Are the ladybugs on this tree identical to each other? How would you investigate this question?

_____

_____

_____

_____

Active Reading

Lesson Vocabulary

List the terms. As you learn about each one, make notes in the Interactive Glossary.

_____

_____

_____

_____

Main Idea and Details

Details give information about a topic. The information may be examples, features, or characteristics. Active readers stay focused on the topic when they ask, What facts or information do these details add to the topic?

Research Is the Key

Tiny insects fly and flash on a summer night. Are you curious about them? Do you wonder how to find out what they are and how they light up? Do some research!

Natural history museums have insect collections as well as scientists who can answer questions about them.

Often scientists ask themselves, "What do other scientists know about this?" To find out, they do *research*. When you research, you use reference materials and talk to experts to learn what is known. So, if you want to learn what scientists know about fireflies, you can do these things:

- Use an encyclopedia.
- Read a book.
- Read science articles.
- Visit a museum.
- E-mail a scientist.
- Visit science websites.

These kinds of resources may have plenty of information about fireflies. But you will still have questions they do not answer. That's when you conduct your own investigations.

Do the Research!

You just saw bees flying in and out of a hole in an old tree. You know it's not a good idea to get too close. So, how can you find out what bees do inside a tree? What research resource would you go to first? Explain why.

_____

_____

_____

_____

Science Tools

What comes to mind when you hear the word *tools*? Hammers, saws, and screwdrivers? How about computers and calculators? Both of these are science tools.

Active Reading As you read these two pages, circle the lesson vocabulary each time it is used.

Scientists use all kinds of tools. Many turn the five senses into "super-senses." Tools enable scientists to see things that are far away, to smell faint odors, to hear quiet sounds, and to feel vibrations their bodies can't.

Let's say you want to observe craters on the moon. A telescope, which makes faraway objects look closer, will turn your sense of sight into "super-vision."

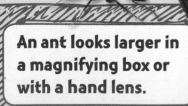

An ant looks larger in a magnifying box or with a hand lens.

What if you're interested in studying tiny critters, such as leaf cutter ants? Take along a hand lens. Hand lenses make small objects look bigger. Is the ant crawling away too fast to see it with the hand lens? Try gently placing the ant in a magnifying box. The top of the box has a lens in it.

Wondering what the ant's bite marks look like? Place a tiny piece of a cut leaf under a microscope. A **microscope** is a tool for looking at objects that cannot be seen with the eye alone.

▶ Predict how the ant would look using a microscope. Make a drawing and add labels.

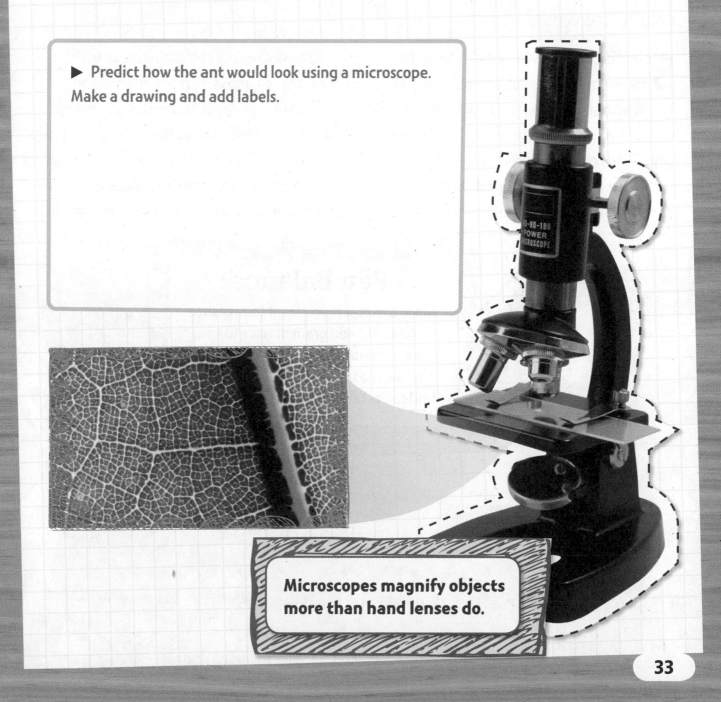

Microscopes magnify objects more than hand lenses do.

Measurement Tools

What's the biggest bug in the world? How far can a grasshopper hop? How long can a butterfly fly? How do scientists find exact answers?

Scientists use measurement tools to make their observations more exact. Think about it this way. You and your friend watch two grasshoppers hop. Your friend says, "This one jumped farther." But you think the other one jumped farther. To find out for sure, you need to measure.

There are tools to measure length or distance, mass, force, volume, and temperature. Most scientists use metric units with these tools. For example, a **pan balance** is used to measure mass with units called grams (g). A **spring scale** is used to measure force in units called newtons (N).

Pan Balance

Place the object you want to measure on one pan. Add gram masses to the other pan until the two pans balance. Add the masses together to find the total in grams (g).

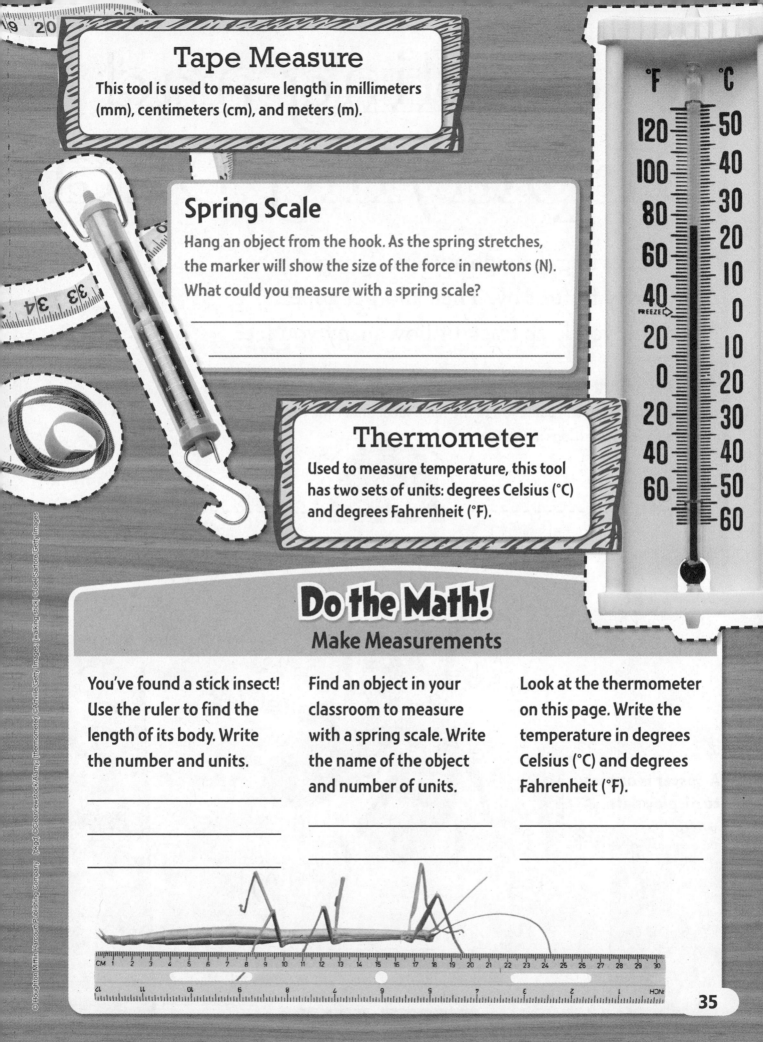

Tape Measure

This tool is used to measure length in millimeters (mm), centimeters (cm), and meters (m).

Spring Scale

Hang an object from the hook. As the spring stretches, the marker will show the size of the force in newtons (N). What could you measure with a spring scale?

_____

_____

Thermometer

Used to measure temperature, this tool has two sets of units: degrees Celsius (°C) and degrees Fahrenheit (°F).

Do the Math!
Make Measurements

You've found a stick insect! Use the ruler to find the length of its body. Write the number and units.

_____

_____

_____

Find an object in your classroom to measure with a spring scale. Write the name of the object and number of units.

_____

_____

Look at the thermometer on this page. Write the temperature in degrees Celsius (°C) and degrees Fahrenheit (°F).

_____

_____

Recording and Displaying Data

You're crawling through a tropical jungle.
A butterfly flutters by. Then another appears.
How will you keep track of how many you see?

A poster is one way to display data.

Recording Data

The bits of information you observe are called **data**. Some data are in the form of numbers. For example, the number of butterflies you see in an hour is a piece of data. Other data are in the form of descriptions. Examples include written notes, diagrams, audio recordings, and photographs.

Only observations are data. So when you think, "There are more butterflies here than in Canada," that's a guess, not data.

Displaying Data

The data you record as you investigate may be correct, but not easy to understand. Later, you can decide how to display the data. For example, you might use your scribbled notes from the jungle to draw a map showing where you saw each butterfly. You might compare the number of each kind of butterfly you found in a circle graph. You might use a bar graph to show the number of butterflies you saw each hour.

Data Two Ways

The table on the left lists six butterflies and the number of wing flaps each one made as it passed by an observer. The bar graph on the right can display the same data. Use the data in the table to complete the graph.

Individual Butterfly	Number of Wing Flaps in a Row
A	3
B	9
C	4
D	3
E	3
F	10

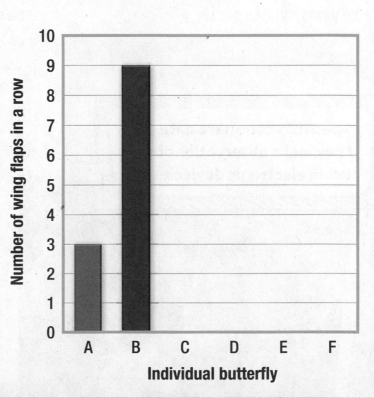

Using Data

You see on the news that the number of honeybees in the United States is decreasing. What is happening to them? How do scientists use data to solve problems and share information?

Drawing Conclusions

You've recorded your data. You've displayed it in a way that is easy to understand. Your next step is to analyze, or look for patterns in, the data. You might identify a trend, or a direction in the data over time. For example, you might conclude that the number of honeybees in your hometown has decreased by 30% in the last five years. What's next?

Communicating

Scientists communicate in many ways. They may work together to collect data. They compare their data with other scientists doing similar investigations. They report their results and conclusions by giving talks and writing reports. Conclusions often lead to new questions to investigate. Scientists are still studying why the number of honeybees is decreasing.

Scientists can share data as they make observations by using electronic devices.

4:25 PM

SEND

Dr. Ruiz,

Just checked the hives on Elm Street. There are many dead bees, and fewer honeycombs than last month.

Dr. Preston

Scientists may work alone or in teams to analyze data and draw conclusions.

► A database is a collection of information or objects. Databases are organized so they are easy to search—like a search website. How would you search a database of insect facts to see what others have learned about the decrease in the number of honeybees?

_____

_____

_____

Museums often have large collections of specimens, so scientists can compare what they have found to what's in a museum.

39

When you're done, use the answer key to check and revise your work.

The outline below is a summary of the lesson. Complete the outline.

Summarize

I. Research Is the Key

   A. Scientists do research to find out what others know.

   B. Reference sources you can use:

      1. encyclopedias

      2. _____

      3. _____

      4. _____

      5. _____

      6. _____

II. Science Tools

   A. Scientists use tools to make the senses more powerful.

   B. Tools that aid the sense of sight:

      1. telescope

      2. _____

      3. _____

      4. _____

III. _____

   A. pan balance

   B. spring scale

   C. tape measure/ruler

   D. _____

IV. Recording and Displaying Data

   A. Data are the bits of information you observe.

   B. Ways to display data:

      1. tables

      2. _____

      3. _____

Word Play

1 Put the mixed-up letters in order to spell a science term from the box.

tada

eama supteer

crasheer

priclg harce

croopsmice

gripes clans

montumceica

axingbynim fog

metermother

lap cannaeb

| circle graph | communicate | data* | magnifying box | microscope* |
| pan balance* | research | spring scale* | tape measure | thermometer |

* Key Lesson Vocabulary

Apply Concepts

2 Someone gives you an object. You think it's a rock, but you aren't sure. Write how you could use each resource to do research.

encyclopedia   websites   books

_____   _____   _____

_____   _____   _____

_____   _____   _____

contact a scientist   museum

_____   _____

_____   _____

_____   _____

3 Draw lines to match the tool to its use.

pan balance   to measure force

spring scale   to look closely at insects outdoors

thermometer   to measure mass

microscope   to find temperature

hand lens   to view objects too small to be seen with the eye alone

Take It Home!

Tell your family about the measurement tools scientists use. Discuss ways your family measures at home. Find and learn to use these tools. Hint: Does your kitchen have tools for measuring foods?

The Nature of Science Students gain scientific knowledge by observing the natural and constructed world, performing and evaluating investigations and communicating their findings. These principles should guide student work and be integrated into the curriculum along with the content standards on a daily basis.

Name _____

Essential Question

Why Do Scientists Compare Results?

Set a Purpose
What will you learn from this investigation?

_____

_____

_____

Think About the Procedure
Which tool will you use to measure mass?

_____

_____

_____

Which units of length will your group use?
Explain your choice.

_____

_____

_____

Record Your Data
In the space below, make a table in which you record your measurements.

Draw Conclusions

Of the three measurement tools you used, which did you find the easiest to use? Which was the hardest? Explain.

_____

_____

_____

_____

Analyze and Extend

1. **Why is it helpful to compare results with others?**

_____

_____

_____

2. **What should you do if you find out that your measurements are very different than those of other teams?**

_____

_____

_____

3. **What other characteristics of the object can you measure?**

_____

_____

_____

4. **The picture shows two more measurement tools. Write about what you could measure with each one.**

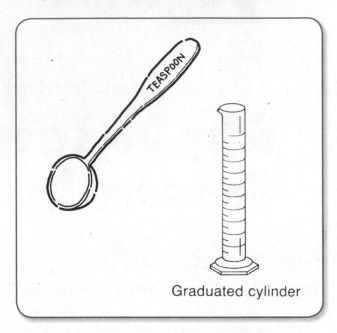

Graduated cylinder

_____

_____

_____

5. **What other questions would you like to ask about science tools?**

_____

_____

_____

_____

44

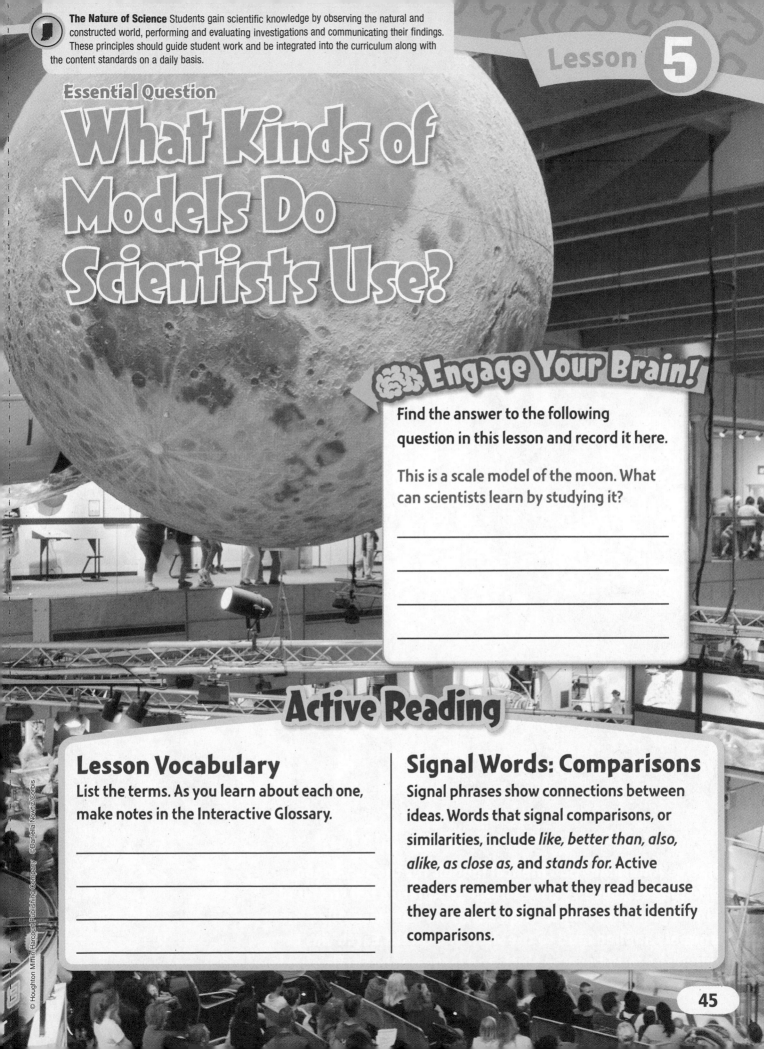

The Nature of Science Students gain scientific knowledge by observing the natural and constructed world, performing and evaluating investigations and communicating their findings. These principles should guide student work and be integrated into the curriculum along with the content standards on a daily basis.

Essential Question

What Kinds of Models Do Scientists Use?

Engage Your Brain!

Find the answer to the following question in this lesson and record it here.

This is a scale model of the moon. What can scientists learn by studying it?

_____

_____

_____

_____

Active Reading

Lesson Vocabulary

List the terms. As you learn about each one, make notes in the Interactive Glossary.

_____

_____

_____

Signal Words: Comparisons

Signal phrases show connections between ideas. Words that signal comparisons, or similarities, include *like, better than, also, alike, as close as,* and *stands for.* Active readers remember what they read because they are alert to signal phrases that identify comparisons.

© Houghton Mifflin Harcourt Publishing Company

Two-dimensional model of the solar system

Models and Science

Native Americans had mental models for the sun, moon, and planets. Several tribes in North America tell stories of the beginning of time, when Earth did not exist. All of the animals applied mud to the shell of a turtle. Earth was born when the mud became thick and large on the turtle's back.

Make a Two-dimensional Model!

Good models are as close to the real thing as possible. Draw a floor plan of a room in your home. Show the doorways and windows. Show the objects that sit on the floor. Add labels. Be as accurate as you can!

A toy car. A doll's house. A person who shows off clothes on a runway. These are all models. But what is a model in science?

Active Reading As you read these two pages, draw a star next to what you think is the most important sentence. Be ready to explain why.

Scientists make models to investigate questions and explain conclusions. In science, a **model** represents something real that is too big, too small, or has too many parts to investigate directly. For example, our solar system is too big to see all the parts at once. So, scientists make models of the solar system. They use models to investigate the motion and positions of planets and moons. They can use the models to predict when a comet or asteroid will pass close to Earth.

Models can take many forms. A *mental model* is a picture you create in your mind. One good thing about this kind of model is that you always have it with you! A **two-dimensional model** has length and width. It can be a drawing, a diagram, or a map.

Other Models Scientists Use

Do the Math!
Use Fractions

You plan to make a model of the solar system. You make the tiniest ball of clay you can for Mercury. The ball is 4 mm across. If Mercury were that size, the chart shows how big all the other objects in your model would be.

Object	Diameter (mm)
Sun	1,100
Mercury	4
Venus	9
Earth	10
Mars	5
Jupiter	110
Saturn	92
Uranus	37
Neptune	36

1. What fraction tells how the size of Mars compares to Earth?

_____

2. Which object is about $\frac{1}{4}$ the diameter of Neptune?

_____

3. Which object is about $\frac{1}{9}$ the diameter of Saturn?

_____

You see thousands of stars in the night sky. You point to a very bright star. Suddenly, you are zooming through space. As you get closer, the star gets bigger and brighter. Your trip isn't real, but it feels like it is. It's another kind of model!

Active Reading As you read these two pages, draw boxes around a clue word or phrase that signal things are being compared.

Three-Dimensional Models

The more a model is like the real thing, the better it is. If the object you want to model has length, width, and height, a **three-dimensional model** is useful. Such a model can show the positions of planets, moons, and the sun better than a two-dimensional model can.

If you want to compare sizes and distances in a model, then you make a *scale model*. The scale tells how much smaller or bigger the model is than the real thing. For example, a model railroad may have a scale of 1 to 48. This means each one inch on the model stands for 48 inches on the real train.

Computer Models

What if you want to understand how asteroids move through the solar system? You'd use a computer model. A **computer model** is a computer program that models an event or object. Some computer models make you feel like you are moving through the solar system!

Weather Models Save Lives

Dangerous weather can happen suddenly. Hurricanes, tornadoes, floods, and winter storms can harm people, pets, and homes. How can models save lives?

FLORIDA

Data from Space

Satellites circle Earth 24 hours each day. Images and other weather data are beamed back to Earth. It's called *real-time* data because scientists see the pictures almost as soon as they are taken. In this image, a hurricane sits along the coast of Florida. The colors are not real. Scientists choose them to show differences in wind speeds, heights of clouds, and other factors.

Using Models

Meteorologists use satellite data to make computer models of weather. They model hurricanes, tornadoes, and thunderstorms. The models are used to predict how and where storms will get started.

This weather model shows the height of the clouds of a storm.

What Can We Do?

You can use models to help your family be prepared for dangerous weather. Draw a diagram of your home in your Science Notebook. Label the exits. Does your family have a safe place to meet in an emergency? Where is it?

_____

_____

_____

_____

How can your model help you in an emergency?

_____

_____

_____

_____

Getting the Word Out

Weather reporters also use models. They make two-dimensional maps for TV and Internet viewers to see. The maps can change to show how fast and where bad weather will be.

Sum It Up!

Use information from the summary to complete the graphic organizer in your own words.

Summarize

For scientists, a model represents something real that is too big, too small, or has too many parts to investigate directly. Scientists use models to investigate and understand the real thing. Several kinds of models are used in science. Two-dimensional models, such as drawings, diagrams, and maps, have length and width. Three-dimensional models have length, width, and height. Computer models are computer programs that behave like the real thing. Some models, such as models of storms, can be used to save lives.

Main Idea: Models in science are like real things and are used to understand real things.

Detail: Two-dimensional models are flat, like a map or a diagram.

Detail: _____ _____ _____

Detail: _____ _____ _____ _____

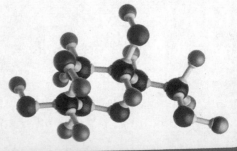

52

Word Play

1 Use the words in the box to complete the puzzle.

computer model*   real-time
mental model   model*
scale model   satellite
two-dimensional model*   weather
three-dimensional model*
*Key Lesson Vocabulary

Across

2. A type of model that is in your head
4. Something that represents the real thing
6. These kinds of models can save lives
7. A type of model that has length and width
9. A device that sends weather images back to Earth

Down

1. A type of model made with a computer program
3. A type of model that has length, width, and height
5. In this type of model, a measurement on the model stands for a measurement on the real thing
8. Data that scientists can see as soon as it is collected

Apply Concepts

Tell how making or using each model below could help people.

2 A model to show where lightning is likely to strike

_____

_____

_____

_____

3 A model to show where water flows during a storm

_____

_____

_____

4 A model to show how traffic moves in a city

_____

_____

5 A model to show equipment for a new playground

_____

_____

Take It Home!

Many kids' toys are models of real things. Challenge your family to find such toys at home, in ads, or where you shop. Ask yourself: How is this toy like the real thing? How is it different?

Name _____

The Nature of Science Students gain scientific knowledge by observing the natural
and constructed world, performing and
evaluating investigations and communicating
their findings. These principles should guide
student work and be integrated into the curriculum along with the content standards on a
daily basis.

Essential Question

How Can You Model a School?

Set a Purpose
What inquiry skills will you practice in this investigation?

_____

_____

_____

Think About the Procedure
How will you decide what part of your school to model?

_____

_____

_____

_____

How will you choose the two types of models?

_____

_____

_____

_____

Record Your Observations
Identify the part of your school you modeled.

_____

_____

_____

Identify the two types of models you made and describe them.

_____

_____

_____

_____

_____

Draw Conclusions

What was something you learned about your school from making the models?

_____

_____

_____

Analyze and Extend

1. Why is it helpful to compare results with others?

_____

_____

_____

2. What was the hardest part of making the models? Explain.

_____

_____

_____

_____

3. Why is it important to be accurate when making your measurements?

_____

_____

_____

4. Why is it important for engineers to make and try out models before making a real building or bridge?

_____

_____

_____

_____

_____

5. What other things or places would you like to learn about by making a model? Explain why.

_____

_____

_____

_____

_____

6. What other questions would you like to ask about making models?

_____

_____

_____

_____

Multiple Choice

1 Luke uses this 2-D model of his classroom on a computer that uses perspective to make it look like a 3-D model.

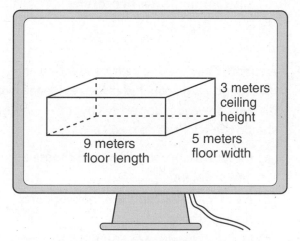

3 meters ceiling height

9 meters floor length

5 meters floor width

He wants to know if the classroom is longer than it is tall. How can he use evidence from this model to answer the question?

(A) He can look at the length of the floor.

(B) He can look at the height of the ceiling.

(C) He can compare the floor length and width.

(D) He can compare the floor length and the ceiling height.

2 A student is studying different types of rocks. Which of the following is something the student must INFER?

(A) the age of the rocks

(B) the mass of the rocks

(C) the color of the rocks

(D) the volume of the rocks

3 Jordan has been observing how well a type of plant grows in different locations. He concludes that a location with bright sunlight is best for the plant. Which of the following could be a reason for his conclusion?

(A) His friend told him that all plants need bright sunlight to grow.

(B) Plants he kept in shade grew better than plants he kept in sunlight.

(C) Plants he kept in shade did not grow as well as plants he kept in sunlight.

(D) He thinks the plants he kept in sunlight would have grown better with more water.

4 A student wants to find out how fast the temperature of water changes when it is under a hot lamp. Which science tools should the student use?

(A) thermometer and clock

(B) meter stick and hand lens

(C) microscope and pan balance

(D) spring scale and tape measure

5 Mia wants to know how fast a ball rolls down a ramp. Which action would BEST help her find this out?

(A) Construct a hypothesis.

(B) Explain why the balls roll so fast.

(C) Observe the ball rolling on the floor.

(D) Measure the ball's speed down the ramp.

6 Different groups of students used a ruler to measure the length of a leaf, as shown below. They recorded the measurements in their science notebooks.

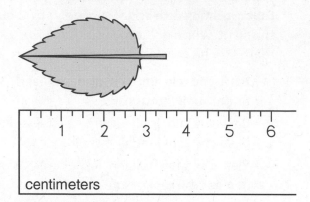

centimeters

Which group recorded the MOST accurate measurement of the leaf?

- (A) Group 1—3.25
- (B) Group 2—3.50 cm
- (C) Group 3—more than 3 cm
- (D) Group 4—between 3 and 4 cm

7 Jake wants to name and describe the parts of an insect to his classmates. Which BEST describes what he should do?

- (A) Make a 3-D model of an insect with clay.
- (B) Have his classmates look at an insect with a hand lens.
- (C) Make a 2-D model of an insect and label its parts.
- (D) Write a report comparing different kinds of insects.

8 A scientist studies a table of data she has collected and recorded. She decides what the results mean and draws a conclusion. What does the scientist do next?

- (A) She makes a prediction.
- (B) She makes a hypothesis.
- (C) She conducts an investigation.
- (D) She communicates her results.

9 A scientist has spent a year conducting an investigation. He concludes that evidence from his work does not support his hypothesis. What should the scientist do next?

- (A) forget this investigation and choose a new problem
- (B) try to make up evidence that supports his hypothesis
- (C) look at the evidence and see if he can make a new hypothesis
- (D) look at the information and find a different way to organize results

10 Grace hypothesizes that hot water will cause a sugar cube to dissolve faster than cold water will. She investigates by filling three cups: one with hot water, one with cold water, and one with ice water. She drops a different number of sugar cubes in each cup. Which BEST describes how Grace could improve the fairness of her investigation?

- (A) She should not have used three cups of water.
- (B) She should have used beakers instead of cups.
- (C) She should have used more variables.
- (D) She should not have two variables that change.

Nature of Science

11 A student builds a clay model to investigate volcanoes. He mixes baking soda and vinegar at the top of his model. When mixed together the baking soda and vinegar fizzle and flow over the top. This reaction makes his volcano appear to erupt. How is the model useful?

Ⓐ It sparks fire like a real volcano.

Ⓑ It shows what a real volcano looks like.

Ⓒ It shoots out material that is hot and then cools.

Ⓓ It models how lava and gases can escape from a volcano.

Nature of Science

12 Raina looks at two models that show how the moon orbits Earth. One model is a computer animation. One model is a diagram. What can Raina do with the computer animation that she cannot do with the diagram?

Ⓐ She can compare the sizes of the moon and Earth.

Ⓑ She can study features of both the moon and Earth.

Ⓒ She can watch the moon in motion as it orbits Earth.

Ⓓ She can get information about the distance between the moon and Earth.

Nature of Science

13 When people think of new ideas, or change an old idea into a different one, they almost always start with some kind of model. They may make other models later on, but which kind of model do they usually start with?

Ⓐ mental model

Ⓑ computer model

Ⓒ two-dimensional model

Ⓓ three-dimensional model

Nature of Science

14 Luis fed his cat in the kitchen. The pictures show what Luis saw as he left the kitchen and then what he saw when he returned.

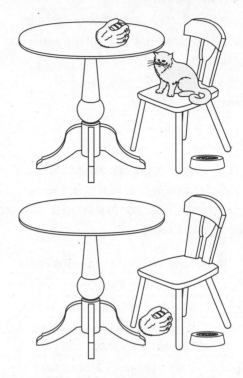

Luis decided the cat jumped on the table and knocked the mitt onto the floor. What scientific skill did Luis use?

Ⓐ He made a hypothesis.

Ⓑ He made an inference.

Ⓒ He made a prediction.

Ⓓ He performed an investigation.

Nature of Science

15 A student wants to find out how much space a small rock takes up. She places water into a graduated cylinder and records the level of water. Then, she adds the rock and measures the level of water again. She calculates the difference in the measurements. What did she find?

Ⓐ the mass of the rock

Ⓑ the weight of the rock

Ⓒ the volume of the rock

Ⓓ the force of the rock

Nature of Science

16 Which of the following is the BEST testable question to investigate in science class?

(A) Why are leaves green?

(B) Does fertilizer help plants grow taller?

(C) Which animal makes a better pet, a dog or a cat?

(D) Why does Jupiter have a ring of frozen gases?

Nature of Science

17 Mrs. Martin challenges her students to identify non-standard tools that will help them measure time. The students' suggestions are recorded in the table below.

Non-standard Measurement Tools

Student	Measuring Tool
Cara	length of time to spell *Mississippi*
Monique	length of time it takes a butterfly to flap its wings once
Ruben	length of time it takes a seed to sprout
Elijah	length of time it takes an ice cube to melt

Which students' suggestion would last about as long as taking a science test?

(A) Cara's suggestion

(B) Monique's suggestion

(C) Ruben's suggestion

(D) Elijah's suggestion

Nature of Science

18 Alex wonders why flowers will not grow in his garden. What part of the scientific process does this represent?

(A) asking a question

(B) making a prediction

(C) drawing a conclusion

(D) conducting an investigation

Nature of Science

19 The local news station asks viewers to measure the amount of rain that falls in their neighborhoods. Four measurements are shown below in milliliter rain gauges.

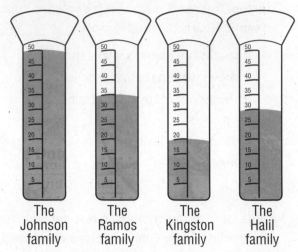

The Johnson family · The Ramos family · The Kingston family · The Halil family

What is the DIFFERENCE between the greatest amount of rain collected and the least amount?

(A) 10 milliliters

(B) 20 milliliters

(C) 30 milliliters

(D) 50 milliliters

Nature of Science

20 Sometimes people use very exact measurements. At other times, it is not as important to be precise. Which activity requires the LEAST exact measurement?

(A) timing a runner trying to break a world record

(B) measuring chemicals for a science investigation

(C) weighing a package to find the price of postage

(D) finding the driving distance between Indianapolis and Chicago

Constructed Response

Nature of Science

21 You are asked to find the average height of five classmates in your class.

Explain what science tool or tools you would need.

_____

How would you find the average?

_____

_____

Nature of Science

22 Frank investigates how a river flowing down a mountain washes away sand, dirt, and soil. Frank builds a pile of sand that resembles a mountain. He observes what happens when he pours a stream of water on the sand pile.

Explain how Frank used a model to investigate the natural world.

_____

_____

_____

Explain why he would do this investigation.

_____

_____

_____

Extended Response

Nature of Science

23 The chart below shows how much a tree grows over 40 years.

Growth of Tree Over 40 years

Time After Planting	Height of Tree in Meters
5 years	1
10 years	3.4
20 years	5.5
30 years	7.2
40 years	7.2

How much did the tree grow between 5 years and 10 years? Between 10 and 20 years? Between 20 and 30 years?

_____

_____

_____

What trend do you see in the data between 5 and 30 years?

_____

Infer why the data for 30 years and 40 years is the same.

_____

Based on the data, what prediction can be made about the height of the tree after 50 years?

_____

_____

Nature of Science

24 It is the annual Egg Drop Day at school. Sophie designs a box that is a 12-cm cube. In her box, she places her egg surrounded by cotton balls. The principal drops all the boxes from the roof. What evidence would prove that Sophie's design failed?

_____

_____

_____

What should Sophie do for the next Egg Drop Day? Describe what would you do to improve her design.

_____

_____

_____

_____

_____

Nature of Science

25 You make a hypothesis that sugar cubes dissolve in hot water faster than in cold water. You decide to test your hypothesis by allowing a sugar cube to dissolve by itself in water at 30 degrees Celsius and another one at 20 degrees Celsius. Your data is shown below.

Time for Sugar Cubes to Dissolve

Trial	20 °C	30 °C
1	1 min 55 sec	45 sec
2	2 min 4 sec	51 sec
3	4 min 2 sec	48 sec

What is the variable that changes in this investigation? What is the variable that must remain the same for all the trials?

_____

_____

In which trial is there probably a mistake in the data? Give a reason that could explain why the data seems incorrect.

_____

_____

_____

Why was the data not exactly the same for each trial? Why was it a good idea to do three trials?

_____

_____

_____

Explain whether the results in the table support the hypothesis.

_____

_____

_____

_____

Heat and Electricity

Indianapolis, Indiana

I Wonder How

Millions of lights twinkle in Indianapolis at night. How are these lights related to giant windmills in the country? *Turn the page to find out.*

Here's How Electricity is produced in energy stations. Some stations burn coal or gas. Others use wind or water power to produce electricity.

Track Your Progress

Essential Questions and Indiana Standards

STANDARD 1
Physical Science

Provide evidence that heat and electricity are forms of energy. Design and assemble electric circuits that provide a means of transferring energy from one form or place to another.

4.1.3 Construct a complete circuit through which an electrical current can pass as evidenced by the lighting of a bulb or ringing of a bell. **4.1.5** Demonstrate that electrical energy can be transformed into heat, light, and sound.

Lesson 1

Essential Question

What Is Electricity?

Engage Your Brain!

As you read the lesson, look for the answer to the following question and record it here.

What causes the girl's hair to stand out from her head?

_____

_____

_____

_____

Active Reading

Lesson Vocabulary

List the terms. As you learn about each one, make notes in the Interactive Glossary.

_____

_____

Main Ideas

The main idea of a paragraph is the most important idea. The main idea may be stated in the first sentence, or it may be stated elsewhere. Active readers look for main ideas by asking themselves, What is this section mostly about?

All Charged Up

You can charge a battery. A football player may charge downfield. How is an electric charge different?

What do you, this book, and your desk have in common? You are all made of atoms. Atoms are the building blocks of all matter. An atom is made of even tinier particles called protons, neutrons, and electrons.

The main difference between protons, electrons, and neutrons is their electric charge. *Electric charge* is a property of a particle that affects how it behaves around other particles.

- Protons have a positive charge (+1).

- Electrons have a negative charge (–1).

- Neutrons are neutral. They have no charge.

When an atom has equal numbers of protons and electrons, the positive charges and negative charges cancel each other. The atom itself has no charge.

Legend

= neutron

= proton

= electron

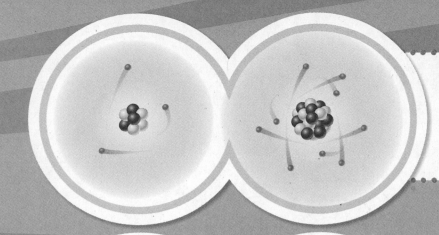

Each of these atoms has equal numbers of protons and electrons. Both atoms are neutral.

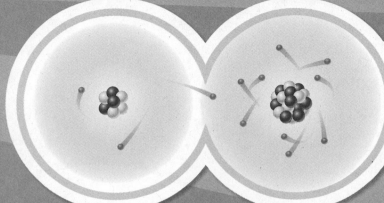

An electron from the atom on the left moves to the atom on the right.

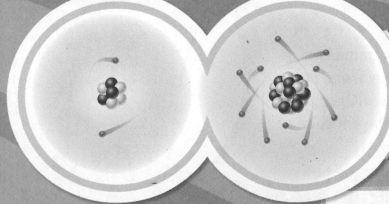

The atom on the left now has a charge of +1. The atom on the right has a charge of –1.

Atoms sometimes gain or lose electrons. Such a gain or loss causes an atom to have an unequal number of positive and negative charges. For example, if an atom with four protons and four electrons gains an electron, the atom will have a charge of –1.

If a neutral atom loses an electron, the number of protons will no longer balance the number of electrons. The atom will have a charge of +1.

▶ Draw an atom with three protons, four neutrons, and four electrons.

What is the charge of the atom?

_____

Opposites Attract

Have you ever had a "bad hair day"? Your hair sticks out in all directions and won't lie flat. What causes that?

Active Reading As you read this page, circle the definitions of *attract* and *repel*. On the next page, draw a box around the sentence with the main idea.

Particles with the same charge repel, or push away from, one another. Particles with opposite charges attract one another, or pull together.

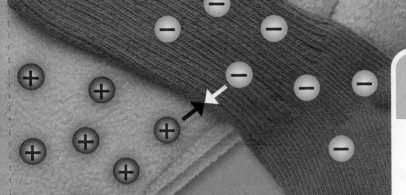

Do the Math!
Positive and Negative Numbers

Fill in the missing squares.

Original Charge on an Object	Electrons Gained or Lost	Final Charge on the Object
+300	Gains 270	
–300	Loses 525	
–270		–500

In the dryer, atoms in clothing gain and lose electrons. Each piece of clothing becomes charged. The positively charged surfaces attract the negatively charged surfaces. As a result, the clothes stick together.

Electric charges can build up on objects. This buildup of charges is called **static electricity**. Objects with opposite electric charges attract each other. Objects with the same charge repel each other.

When you brush your hair, electrons move from each strand of hair to the brush. Soon all the strands are positively charged. Having the same charge causes the strands to repel one another and stick out.

A charged object can also attract a neutral object. If you rub a balloon on your hair, the balloon picks up extra electrons. They give it a negative charge. When you bring the balloon near a wall, electrons in a small section of the wall are repelled and move away. This leaves a positive charge at the surface of the wall. The balloon sticks to the wall.

Lightning Strikes

Thunderstorms can be scary. Lightning strikes can be deadly. What is lightning, and how can you stay safe during a thunderstorm?

Active Reading As you read these two pages, underline the main idea on each page.

Static electricity is a buildup of charges on an object. The word *static* means "not moving." Charges stay on an object until it comes close to an object with a different charge.

As you walk across a carpet, electrons move from the carpet to you. Because electrons repel each other, they spread out all over your body. When you touch something, the electrons jump from your finger to the object. This jumping is called an electrostatic discharge. You feel it as a tiny shock.

ZAP!
Electrons jump from a person with a negative charge.

▶ Complete this cause-and-effect graphic organizer.

Cause: An object with a negative charge is placed near an object with a positive charge.	→	Effect: _____ _____ _____

Not all electrostatic discharges cause small shocks. Some result in huge shocks. During a thunderstorm, tiny raindrops or ice particles bump into each other. These collisions cause an electric charge to build in the clouds.

Positive charges form at the top of a cloud and on the ground. Negative charges form near the bottom of a cloud. When the difference in charge between a cloud and the ground is great enough, there is a huge electrostatic discharge that we call lightning.

A lightning spark can jump between two clouds, between a cloud and air, or between a cloud and the ground. The temperature inside a lightning bolt can reach 50,000 °F. That's hotter than the surface of the sun!

Lightning Safety

- Stay inside during thunderstorms.

- Turn off electrical appliances and stay away from windows.

- If you can't get inside a safe place, wait in a car with a metal top for the storm to pass.

- Know the weather forecast. If you will be outdoors, have a plan in case a thunderstorm develops.

Objects that lightning strikes can catch on fire. A tree struck by lightning may split.

Current Events

You can control electrons by making them flow through a wire in the way water flows in a river.

When electric charges have a path to follow, as they do in the wire below, they move in a steady flow. This flow of charges is called an electric current.

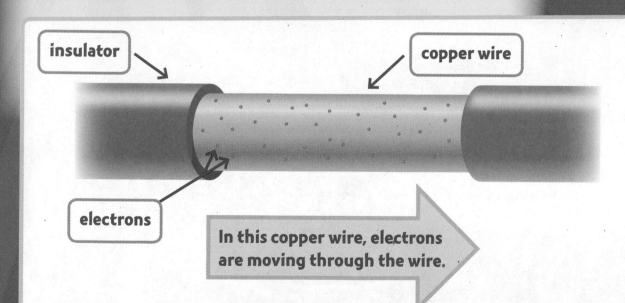

insulator

copper wire

electrons

In this copper wire, electrons are moving through the wire.

Chemical reactions in a battery provide the energy that causes the electrons to flow. An energy station is another source of electric current.

▶ What do the blue dots on this wire represent, and what is it called when they flow?

_____

_____

_____

© Houghton Mifflin Harcourt Publishing Company (t) ©Jim Goldstein/Alamy

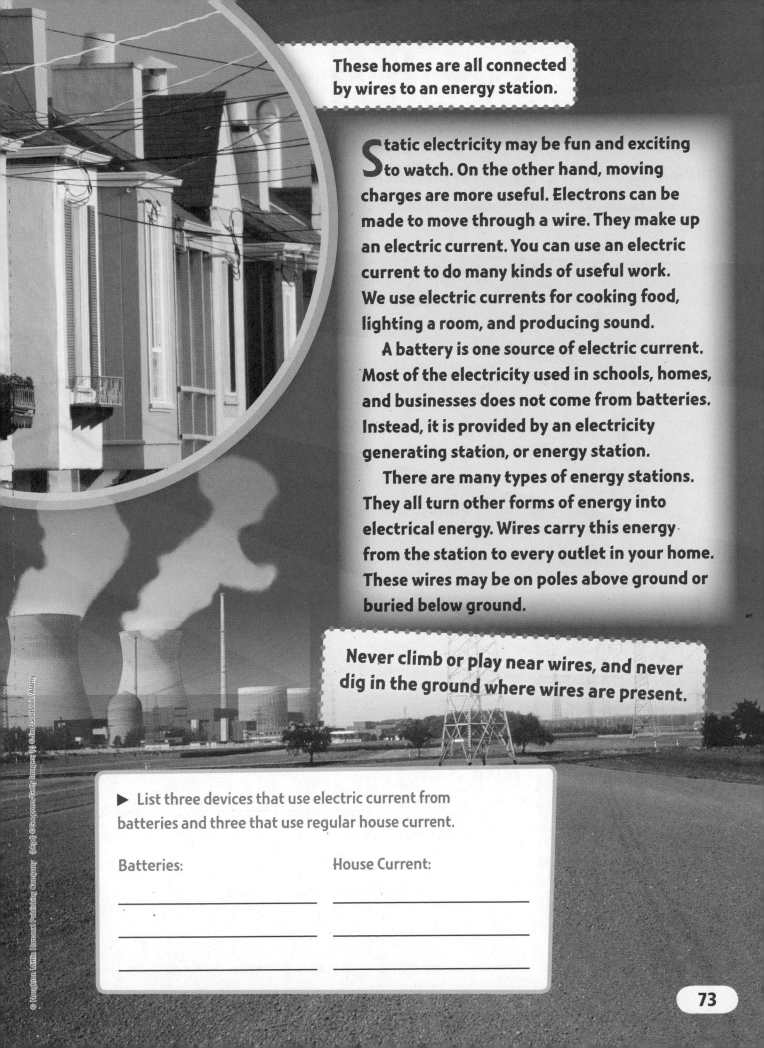

These homes are all connected by wires to an energy station.

Static electricity may be fun and exciting to watch. On the other hand, moving charges are more useful. Electrons can be made to move through a wire. They make up an electric current. You can use an electric current to do many kinds of useful work. We use electric currents for cooking food, lighting a room, and producing sound.

A battery is one source of electric current. Most of the electricity used in schools, homes, and businesses does not come from batteries. Instead, it is provided by an electricity generating station, or energy station.

There are many types of energy stations. They all turn other forms of energy into electrical energy. Wires carry this energy from the station to every outlet in your home. These wires may be on poles above ground or buried below ground.

Never climb or play near wires, and never dig in the ground where wires are present.

▶ List three devices that use electric current from batteries and three that use regular house current.

Batteries:

House Current:

_____   _____

_____   _____

_____   _____

Sum It Up!

When you're done, use the answer key to check and revise your work.

The outline below is a summary of the lesson. Complete the outline.

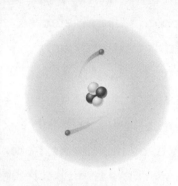

I. Electric Charges

    A. Each of the three types of particles that make up atoms has a different charge.

        1. Protons have a positive charge.

        2. _____

        3. _____

    B. Atoms can gain or lose electrons.

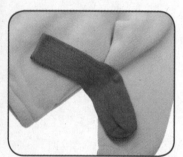

II. Static Electricity

    A. Definition: the buildup of electric charge on an object

    B. Objects with charges interact with each other.

        1. Like charges repel.

        2. _____

III. Electrostatic Discharge

    A. Definition: the jumping of electrons from one object to another

    B. Examples

        1. Getting shocked after walking across a rug

        2. _____

IV. Electric Current

    A. Definition: _____

    B. Sources

        1. _____

        2. Electricity generating stations

Answer Key: I. A. 2. Electrons have a negative charge. I. A. 3. Neutrons have no charge. II. B. 2. Opposite charges attract. III. B. 2. Lightning IV. A. the flow of electrons through a wire. IV. B. 1. Batteries

Brain Check

Lesson **1**

Name _____

Word Play

1 Fill in the blank in each sentence. Then find the words in the blanks in the word search.

a. Two positive charges _____ each other.

b. A positive charge and a negative charge _____ each other.

c. The buildup of electric charge on an object is _____ electricity.

d. The steady flow of electric charges along a path is electric _____.

e. A proton has a _____ charge.

f. A neutron is _____ because it has no charge.

g. An electron has a _____ charge.

h. Electricity is produced at a generating _____.

```
C  N  E  G  A  T  I  V  E
U  F  R  E  P  E  L  R  V
R  I  G  H  T  E  N  I  I
R  N  A  T  T  R  A  C  T
E  G  C  I  T  A  T  S  I
N  E  U  T  R  A  L  L  S
T  I  G  H  T  N  I  N  O
S  T  A  T  I  O  N  G  P
```

Find the letters you didn't circle in the word search. Write them in order from left to right in the blanks below.

Riddle: What do you call a very scary electrostatic discharge?

__ __ __ __ __ __ __ __ __   __ __ __ __ __ __ __ __ __

© Houghton Mifflin Harcourt Publishing Company

75

Apply Concepts

2 List the three particles that make up an atom. Describe the charge of each particle.

Parts of an Atom	
Particle	Charge

Where are these particles found in an atom?

_____

_____

_____

3 Draw an atom with 9 protons, 10 neutrons and a charge of −1. Label each part in your drawing.

4 Explain why the balloons are sticking to this cat.

_____

_____

_____

_____

5 Look at the pairs of objects below. The charge of each object is shown. Tell how each pair will interact. Write *attract*, *repel*, or *nothing*.

+22	−34	_____
0	+130	_____
−40	−81	_____
0	0	_____

6 Complete the sequence graphic organizer.

A wool sock and a cotton shirt _____ against each other in a dryer.

↓

Electrons move from the wool to the _____ .

↓

The two pieces of clothing have _____ charges and they _____ each other.

7 List three ways in which electric current helps you do work, and describe the energy transformation that takes place.

_____

_____

_____

_____

_____

_____

_____

_____

8 Explain why the event in the drawing takes place.

_____

_____

_____

_____

_____

_____

_____

9 Match each drawing with its description. Circle the drawings that show sources of current that people use every day.

electric current	static electricity	electrostatic discharge	battery

10 Suppose you are playing soccer at a park and you hear thunder that sounds far away. Describe some things you should and should not do to stay safe.

_____

_____

_____

_____

_____

_____

Take It Home! Do your clothes stick together when they come out of the dryer? If so, how could you prevent this from happening? If not, why don't they stick together? When you put on a sweater, does it ever stick to your hair? Does this happen throughout the year, or only at certain times?

4.1.3 Construct a complete circuit through which an electrical current can pass as evidenced by the lighting of a bulb or ringing of a bell. **4.1.4** Experiment with materials to identify conductors and insulators of heat and electricity.

Essential Question

What Are Electric Circuits, Conductors, and Insulators?

Engage Your Brain!

Find the answer to the following question and record it here.

This picture shows the inside of a robot. What do the dark lines have to do with the robot's operation?

_____

_____

_____

_____

Active Reading

Lesson Vocabulary

List the terms. As you learn about each one, make notes in the Interactive Glossary.

_____ _____

_____ _____

_____

Compare and Contrast

When you compare things, you look for ways in which they are alike. When you contrast things, you look for ways in which they are different. As you read each page, look for ways in which the things described are alike and different.

It's Shocking!

Working around electric utility lines is dangerous! How does a line worker avoid getting hurt?

Active Reading Draw a box around the sentences that contrast conductors and insulators.

Even on a hot day, a worker who repairs electric utility lines is bundled up in protective clothing. The thick gloves, the bulky boots, and the hard plastic hat are very heavy. But they help to keep the worker from being electrocuted!

The rubber and plastic used in protective clothing do not allow the flow of electric charge. A material that resists the flow of electric charge is called an **insulator**.

Electric charges flow easily through metals and some liquids. A material that readily allows electric charges to pass through it is called a **conductor**.

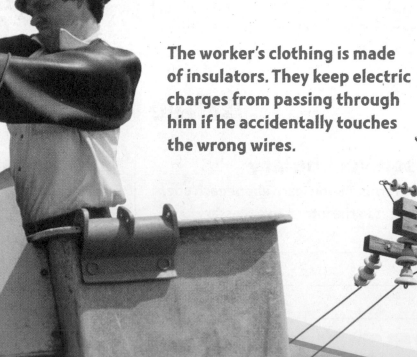

The worker's clothing is made of insulators. They keep electric charges from passing through him if he accidentally touches the wrong wires.

The parts that you hold on a plug, as well as the covering of the wire, are insulators. The metal prongs that go into the outlet are good conductors.

Electrical appliances work when electric charges flow through them. The parts that carry electric charges are made of conductors. Insulators are wrapped around the conductors, making the appliances safe to handle.

▶ Label the parts by writing *conductor* or *insulator*.

_____

_____

▶ Why are insulators used?

_____

_____

_____

_____

_____

_____

_____

A Path to Follow

The wiring in a lamp doesn't change. So why isn't the light on all the time?

Active Reading Draw a box around sentences that tell you how a closed circuit and an open circuit differ.

When you go to school and back home, your path is a loop. An electric **circuit** is a path along which electric charges can flow. For an electrical device to work, the circuit must form a complete loop. This type of circuit is called a *closed circuit*. There are no breaks in the path.

What happens if a loose wire gets disconnected? The path is broken, and charges cannot flow. This type of circuit is called an *open circuit*. Many circuits have a switch. A switch controls the flow of charges by opening and closing the circuit.

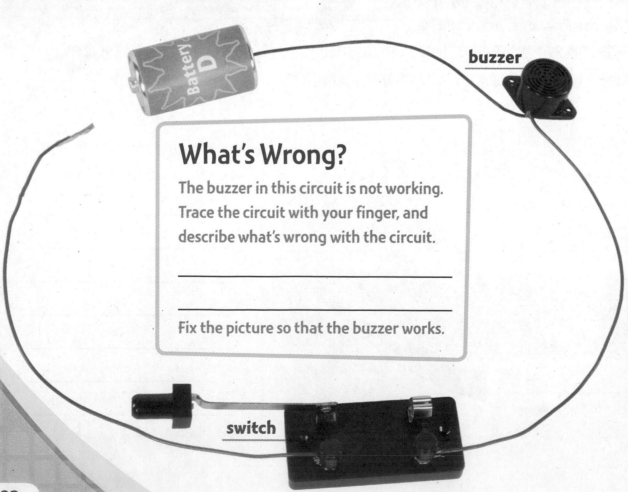

buzzer

What's Wrong?

The buzzer in this circuit is not working. Trace the circuit with your finger, and describe what's wrong with the circuit.

_____

_____

Fix the picture so that the buzzer works.

switch

Open Circuit

When the switch in a circuit is open, the circuit isn't complete. Electric charges cannot flow, so the light stays off.

Closed Circuit

The switch is now closed. Electric charges can flow through the circuit, and the bulb lights up.

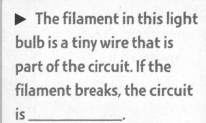

▶ The filament in this light bulb is a tiny wire that is part of the circuit. If the filament breaks, the circuit is _____.

filament

Who Needs a Map?

To travel from point A to point B, you usually take the shortest route. What if one of the roads on that route is blocked? Simple! You just take another road. But what would happen if there were only one road from point A to point B?

Active Reading Underline the sentences that compare series circuits and parallel circuits.

Series Circuits

In a series circuit, electric charges must follow a single path. The charged particles move from the battery's positive terminal to its negative terminal.

▶ Draw an arrow showing how charges flow in this circuit.

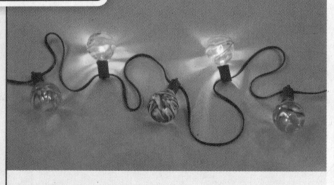

If one light bulb in a series circuit burns out, all of the lights go out because the circuit is broken.

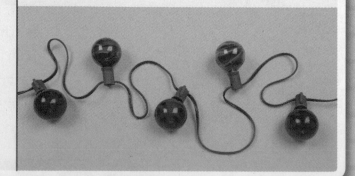

Suppose that the television and all the lights in a room are part of the same circuit. What would happen if one of the light bulbs burned out? It would depend on how the circuit is wired.

A **series circuit** has only one path for electric charges to follow. If any part of the path breaks, the circuit is open. Nothing works!

A circuit with several different paths for the charges to follow is called a **parallel circuit**. If one part of the circuit breaks, the charges can still flow along the other parts.

Color a Complex Circuit

1. Look at the circuit below. Color the bulb or bulbs that should be lit.
2. Draw an *X* on the switch that is open. Draw an arrow above the closed switch.

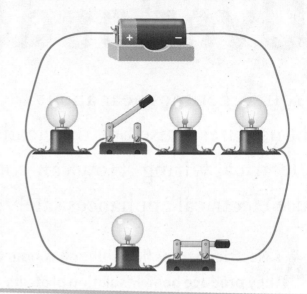

Parallel Circuits

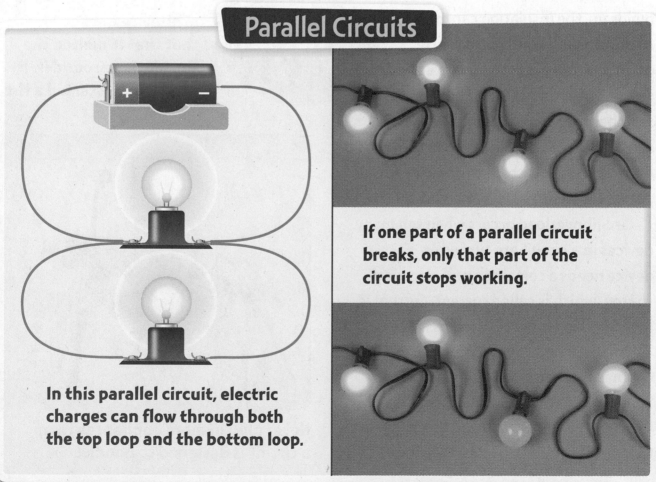

In this parallel circuit, electric charges can flow through both the top loop and the bottom loop.

If one part of a parallel circuit breaks, only that part of the circuit stops working.

Circuit Overload!

You sometimes hear about house fires caused by overloaded electrical wiring. How can you use electrical appliances safely?

television
3 amps

hair dryer
12.5 amps

As electric charges flow through conductors, they produce heat. Insulation protects the materials around it from the heat —up to a point! If too much heat builds up, the insulation can melt. As protection against fires, a fuse or a circuit breaker is added to each circuit. Fuses and circuit breakers are switches that work automatically. They open if charge flows too quickly through a circuit. The flow stops and the wires cool, preventing a fire.

Circuit overload occurs when too many devices in a circuit are turned on. Each device needs a certain flow of electrical charge, which is called current. Current is measured in amperes, or amps (A).

Circuit breakers open when the number of amps is greater than a certain value. Suppose the value for a breaker is 15 A. In this case, all the devices you use at the same time must require no more than 15 A.

WOW!

This wire got so hot that it melted the insulation around it. It could have started a fire.

Never plug in more appliances than a circuit is designed to handle!

86

Should You Plug It In?

Draw a line connecting the hair dryer to one of the outlets in the power strip. Then connect the other devices you could use at the same time without overloading a 15-amp circuit breaker.

With power strips like this one, it's possible to plug many devices into a single wall outlet. **That could be a big mistake!**

lava lamp
0.5 amp

laptop computer
1.5 amps

clothes dryer
42 amps

This panel contains circuit breakers. Each breaker allows a certain number of amps of electric current to pass through one circuit.

Do the Math!
Solve Word Problems

1. How many times more amps does a television need than a lava lamp?

_____

2. Circuit breakers are made in increments of 5 amps. What size breaker would you need for a circuit with a television, two laptops, and a lava lamp?

_____

Sum It Up!

When you're done, use the answer key to check and revise your work.

On each numbered line, fill in the vocabulary term that matches the description.

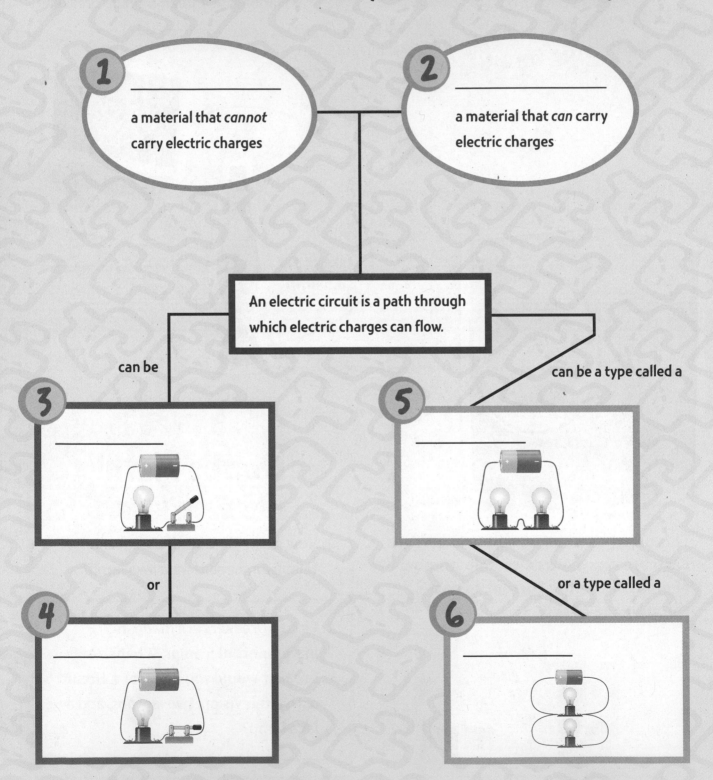

1 _____

a material that *cannot* carry electric charges

2 _____

a material that *can* carry electric charges

An electric circuit is a path through which electric charges can flow.

can be

3 _____

or

4 _____

can be a type called a

5 _____

or a type called a

6 _____

Name _____

Word Play

1 Unscramble the scrambled word in each sentence. Write the unscrambled word after the sentence. The first one is done for you.

a. In some circuits, electrical energy is transformed into light energy by a light **lubb**.	(B)U L B 6
b. The wires in a circuit are made of a material that is a **doortuccn**.	_ _ _ _ _ _ _ _ ◯ 10
c. A path that electricity can follow is an electric **icurict**.	_ _ _ _ ◯ ◯ _ 4 5
d. A circuit in which electric charges can follow several different paths is called a **rallpale** circuit.	◯ _ _ _ _ _ _ 8
e. If a wire is disconnected, the circuit is an **enop** circuit.	_ ◯ _ _ 9
f. The covering on electric plugs and around wires is made of an **rainulost**.	◯ _ _ _ _ _ _ ◯ 2 7
g. A circuit in which all the devices are connected in a single path is a **ressie** circuit.	_ ◯ _ _ _ 3
h. When a light is on, it is part of a **scolde** circuit.	◯ _ _ _ _ _ 1

Solve the riddle by writing the circled letters above in the correct spaces below.

Riddle: What is another name for a clumsy electrician?

A _ _ _ _ C _ I _   B _ E _ K _ _ _
1 2 3   4 5   6 7   8   9 10

Apply Concepts

2 Draw an open series circuit with two light bulbs, a battery, and a switch.

3 Explain what an overloaded circuit is. How can you prevent having an overloaded circuit?

_____

_____

_____

_____

_____

_____

4 Write the word *conductor* or *insulator* on each of the lines. Then infer which type of material is inside the holes in the outlet. Explain.

_____

_____

_____

5 Suppose you are building a series circuit with a battery and a small light bulb and you run out of wire. What common objects could you use to connect the battery to the light bulb? Explain.

_____

_____

_____

6 Name each lettered part of the circuit, and explain what the part does.

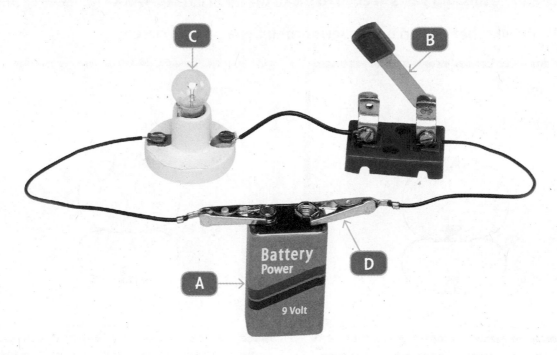

A _____

B _____

C _____

D _____

7 Many appliances in your home use electrical energy. What other forms of energy are produced when the appliances are turned on? Name at least three different appliances and the types of energy they produce.

_____

_____

_____

_____

8 Study each of the following circuits.

- Make a check mark to show whether the circuit is open or closed.

- Draw the missing parts needed to make the open circuits work.

- Write whether the circuit is a series circuit or a parallel circuit.

☐ open
☐ closed

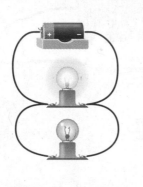

_____

☐ open
☐ closed

_____

☐ open
☐ closed

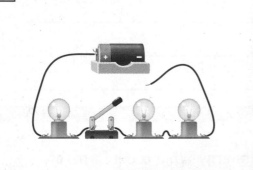

_____

☐ open
☐ closed

_____

Take It Home!

Discuss with your family what you have learned about circuits. Gather some electrical devices and explain how they use electricity. Try flipping some switches in your home, and explain whether they are series circuits or parallel circuits.

4.1.3 Construct a complete circuit through which an electrical current can pass as evidenced by the lighting of a bulb or ringing of a bell. 4.1.4 Experiment with materials to identify conductors and insulators of heat and electricity. **Nature of Science**

Name _____

Essential Question

How Can You Construct an Electric Circuit?

Set a Purpose
What will you learn from this investigation?

_____

_____

_____

_____

Think About the Procedure
Did the order in which you arranged the parts make a difference? Explain.

_____

_____

_____

_____

Was the procedure an experiment? Why or why not?

_____

_____

_____

Record Your Data
In the space below, draw your circuit that worked. Label each part, and describe how the parts were connected.

Place a check mark next to the materials that enabled the bulb to light up.

Paper clip _____

Wood craft stick _____

Pencil lead _____

Draw Conclusions

How can you build a circuit?

_____

_____

_____

_____

_____

Analyze and Extend

1. Why is it helpful to have a switch in a circuit?

_____

_____

_____

_____

2. Why would a circuit not work when a wire is replaced with a cotton string?

_____

_____

_____

3. Look at the first part of the word *circuit*. Why do you think what you built is called a circuit?

_____

_____

_____

4. Look at the drawing below. Draw lines to show how three wires could be connected to make the bulbs light up.

5. Each part of a circuit has a different job. Write the name of the part that performs each job below.

- Source of current _____
- Carries current _____
- Turns circuit on and off _____
- Changes electrical energy to light _____

6. What other questions would you like to ask about electric circuits? What investigations could you do to answer the questions?

_____

_____

_____

_____

_____

_____

_____

Essential Question

How Do We Use Electricity?

🧠 Engage Your Brain!

As you read, figure out the answer to the following question and record it here.

How would this scene have been different in 1910?

_____

_____

_____

Active Reading

Lesson Vocabulary

List the terms. As you learn about each one, make notes in the Interactive Glossary.

_____

_____

Signal Words: Sequence

Signal words show connections between ideas. Words that signal sequence include *now, before, after, first,* and *next.* Active readers remember what they read because they look for signal words that identify sequence.

Electricity
Has Many Uses

Suppose you had lived in 1900 rather than today. The pictures show how different your day might have been.

Active Reading As you read this page, write *before* or *after* in the box next to each object to indicate the sequence.

Does a clock radio wake you up in the morning? Do you use an electric toothbrush or hair dryer? How do you cook your breakfast?

Electrical appliances do work. They perform useful tasks by converting electrical energy into other forms of energy, such as sound, thermal, and mechanical energy. Some appliances run on batteries. Others are plugged into a socket, which provides greater electrical energy. Think about the appliances you use each day. How would your day change if there were no electricity?

The only light came from candles or oil-burning lamps. Now we can turn on lamps with the flick of a switch.

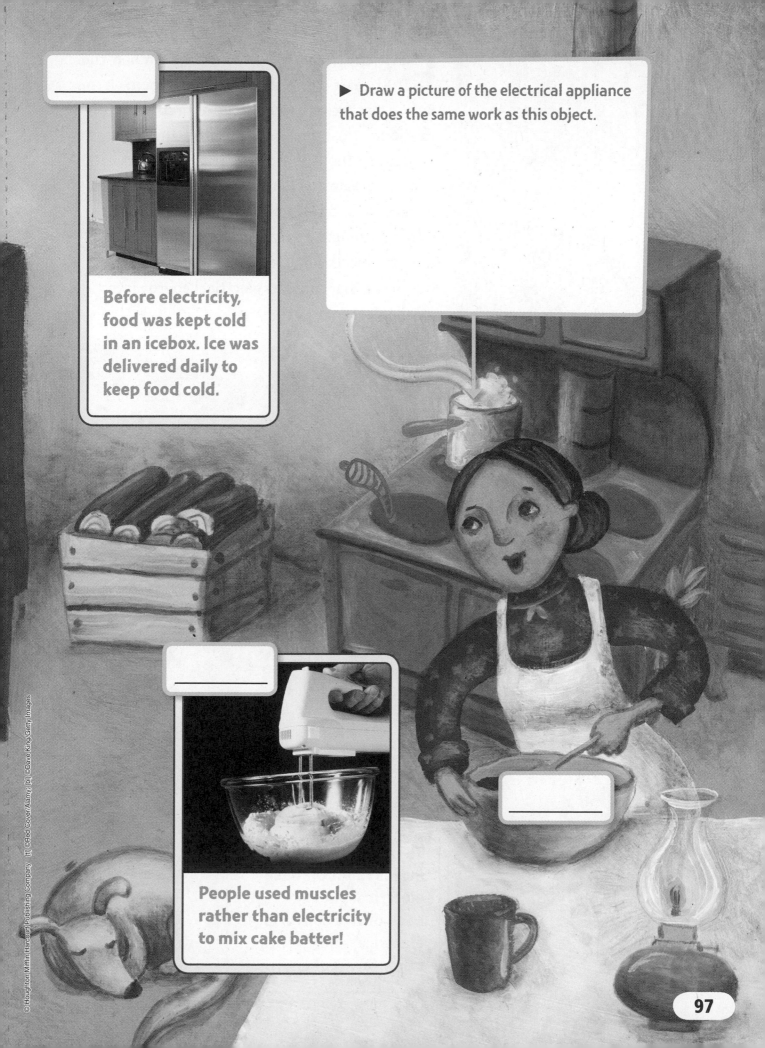

_____

Before electricity, food was kept cold in an icebox. Ice was delivered daily to keep food cold.

▶ Draw a picture of the electrical appliance that does the same work as this object.

_____

People used muscles rather than electricity to mix cake batter!

_____

Electricity changed life outside the kitchen, too. The heater in this scene keeps the room warm. Before electricity, a wood stove or fireplace heated the home. Cleaning was harder, too. There were no vacuum cleaners. There was no television to watch or radio to listen to. People entertained themselves by reading or by playing cards.

Many modern appliances, such as mixers and fans, use electric motors. An **electric motor** is a device that converts electrical energy into mechanical energy.

electric heater

There are many devices in this room that use electrical energy. Each device converts electrical energy into other forms of energy.

Then and Now

Match the objects that do the same kind of work. Draw a picture of the missing appliance. Then describe the energy change that takes place in each electrical appliance.

Electromagnets

Electricity and magnetism are related.
One can produce the other.

Active Reading As you read this page, circle the sentence that explains how magnetism produces an electric current.

Suppose you slide a coil of wire back and forth around a bar magnet. When the ends of the wire are attached to a light bulb, the bulb lights! Moving a magnet and a wire near each other produces an electric current.

Turning the handle on the device below turns a coil of wire inside three U-shaped magnets. Electricity flows through the wire and lights the lamp.

Hand-cranked light bulb

Modern hand-cranked flashlight

If magnets produce electricity, can electricity make magnets? Yes! Wrapping a coil of current-carrying wire around an iron nail makes the nail a magnet. You can use it to pick up small iron objects such as paper clips. A device in which current produces magnetism is called an **electromagnet**.

Huge electromagnets are used in junk yards. They separate iron and steel objects from other objects. The operator swings the electromagnet over a pile of junk. He turns on the current. All the iron pieces jump to the magnet. The operator then swings the magnet over a container and turns off the current. The magnetism stops, and the iron drops into the container.

Electromagnets have become very important and useful. Every electric motor today contains at least one electromagnet. You can also find electromagnets in telephones, doorbells, speakers, and computers. Doctors can use electromagnets to make pictures of the inside of the body.

▶ In the first box, write the cause of the action in the second box. Then figure out what that effect can cause, and fill in the third box.

_____ _____ _____ _____	An electric current flows through the wire.	_____ _____ _____

Conserving Electricity

You've probably been asked to conserve, or use less, electricity. Why is conserving electricity important?

Active Reading As you read, underline a sentence that tells how you can conserve energy.

hydroelectric dam

Inside a hydroelectric [hy•droh•ee•LEK•trik] dam, the mechanical energy of falling water is used to turn generators, which change mechanical energy into electrical energy.

Electricity generating stations, also known as energy stations, may use water, coal, or atoms to produce the electricity you use.

windmills

Windmills have been used to grind grain or pump water. Today, wind turbines generate electricity.

Suppose you spin a magnet inside a coil of wire. A current flows through the wire. You've made a **generator**, a device that converts kinetic energy to electrical energy. Huge generators in energy stations change kinetic energy into electricity. The electricity travels through wires to homes, schools, and businesses.

Some energy stations use falling water or wind to turn generators. Other energy stations convert solar energy to electricity. These resources will never run out. They are called renewable resources.

Most energy stations burn coal or other fuels to heat water. The water rises as steam, which turns the generator. Coal is a limited resource. It will eventually run out. That's why it is important to conserve, or use less, electricity. For example, you can turn off the lights when you leave a room or use a towel instead of a hair dryer.

Do the Math!
Solve a Problem

Sam's electric bill was $200 for the month of June. The air conditioner accounts for $\frac{1}{2}$ of the bill, and the water heater accounts for $\frac{1}{5}$ of the bill. How much did it cost to run each appliance in June?

103

Use information in the summary to complete the graphic organizer.
When you're done, use the answer key to check and revise your work.

Summarize

Electrical appliances use electrical energy to do work and perform useful tasks. Some of these appliances, such as a flashlight or an MP3 player, get electricity from batteries. Others must be plugged into a wall socket. Electrical appliances convert electrical energy into other forms of energy, such as thermal energy, sound energy, and light energy. Many appliances, such as washing machines and fans, contain an electric motor, which converts electricity into the energy of motion. An electric current may also be used to make an electromagnet. Generators in energy stations produce electric current, which travels through wires to homes, schools, and businesses. It is important to conserve electricity because some of the resources energy stations use will eventually run out.

1 Main Idea: Electrical appliances use electrical energy to

_____

_____

2 Detail: Some appliances work on batteries. Others must be

_____

_____

_____

_____

3 Detail: Electrical appliances convert

_____

_____

_____

_____

4 Detail: Conserving electricity is important because

_____

_____

_____

_____

Answer Key: 1. do work and perform useful tasks. 2. plugged into a wall socket. 3. electrical energy to other forms of energy, such as thermal, sound, light, and mechanical energy. 4. Some resources used by energy stations will run out.

Word Play

1 Unscramble each of the clues to form a word or a phrase from the word bank. Copy each letter in a numbered cell to the cell below with the same number.

TECGARLOETNEM [ ][ ][ ][ ][ ][ ][ ][ ][ ][5][ ][ ][ ]

RECLICTE ROOTM [ ][ ][8][ ][ ][ ][ ][ ] [ ][ ][ ][ ][ ]

TORRAGEEN [ ][ ][4][ ][ ][ ][ ][ ]

ONECREVS [ ][ ][ ][2][ ][ ][ ][ ]

REECUSROS [ ][ ][ ][ ][1][ ][ ][ ][ ]

GANSEITMM [ ][ ][10][7][ ][ ][3][ ][ ]

CICLETERTIY [6][ ][ ][ ][ ][9][ ][ ][ ][ ][11]

Word Bank
conserve
electricity
electric motor
electromagnet
generator
magnetism
resources

This lesson is about [1][2][3][4][5] [6][7][8][9][10][11] .

Apply Concepts

2 Draw a common electrical appliance. Then explain how it changes electrical energy to other forms of energy and what kind of work it does.

_____

_____

_____

_____

3 Draw an *X* over each appliance that changes electrical energy to mechanical energy.

Circle each appliance that changes electrical energy to thermal energy.

Draw a square around each appliance that changes electrical energy to sound energy.

Draw a triangle around each appliance that changes electrical energy to light energy.

4 What is the device in this drawing called? What would happen if you put this device near a pile of iron nails? Why?

_____

_____

_____

5 A. What are some resources used to generate electricity in energy stations?

_____

_____

B. Describe three ways that you can conserve electricity.

_____

_____

_____

_____

_____

Take It Home!

Discuss with your family some specific ways that you could conserve electricity. You might talk about ways to use less electricity or about things you can do by hand rather than using an electrical appliance.

106

Careers in Science

Ask an Electrician

Q. Do electricians make electricity?

A. No. Electricity is produced in energy stations and carried to buildings through wires. Electricians work with wires to make sure the electricity moves safely.

Q. Don't electricians worry about electric shocks when they work?

A. Electricians must always turn off electricity to the wires they are working on. Electricity can be dangerous and safety is an important part of the job.

Q. What kind of training do you need to be an electrician?

A. Most electricians learn from experienced electricians while they are attending classes. During this time, they are called apprentices.

Now It's Your Turn!

What question would you ask an electrician?

_____

_____

_____

_____

Untangle the Wires!

For each circuit, explain what would happen
when the switch at the bottom is closed.

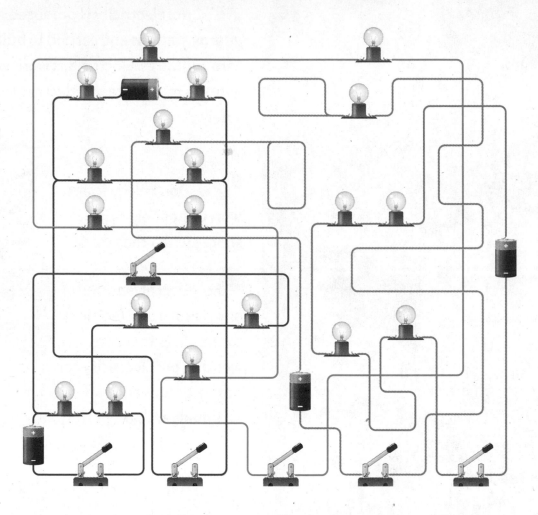

Red: _____

Purple: _____

Green: _____

Orange: _____

Blue: _____

Essential Question

What Is Heat?

Engage Your Brain!

Find the answer to the following question in this lesson and record it here.

What is the difference between the body of this ice skater and the ice around her?

_____

_____

_____

_____

Active Reading

Lesson Vocabulary

List the terms. As you learn about each one, make notes in the Interactive Glossary.

_____

_____

_____

_____

Signal Words: Contrast

Signal words show connections between ideas. Words that signal contrasts include *unlike, different from, but,* and *on the other hand.* Active readers remember what they read because they are alert to signal words that identify contrasts.

A Hot Topic!

What makes fresh toast feel hot and ice feel cold? Heat. But how can the same thing cause two different sensations?

Active Reading As you read these two pages, find and underline the definition of *heat*.

You have learned that electricity is a form of energy. Heat is another form of energy. **Heat** is the energy that moves between objects of different temperatures. Temperature is the way we measure how hot or cold something is. Energy in the form of heat moves from warmer objects to cooler objects.

When you touch something that is warmer than your skin, you sense the heat energy as a warming feeling. You feel the change in temperature as you gain energy. When you touch something that is cooler than your skin, you sense heat moving from your body into the cooler object.

Super Hot

You can see and feel heat moving from the flame to the glass. This melted glass is about 1,500 °C (2,732 °F)!

Incredibly Cold

This is dry ice—frozen carbon dioxide. It is really cold—about –80 °C (–112 °F).

Do the Math!
Use Temperature Scales

Temperature is measured in different scales. The two scales on this thermometer are Celsius and Fahrenheit. Write the letter of each picture at the appropriate place on the thermometer.

A

This girl's clothes trap heat near her body. Her jacket slows down energy transfer to the cold air. This girl stays warm while playing in the snow in temperatures as low as 0 °C (32 °F).

B

The water coming from this shower head is hotter than the air around it. The average temperature of shower water is about 42 °C (108 °F).

C

Ice cubes melt as energy transfers to them from the warm air. The puddle of water is about 10 °C (50 °F).

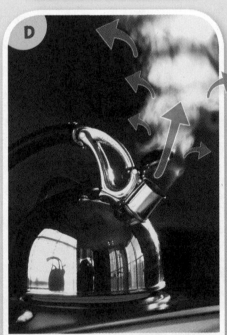

D

Energy moves from the burner to the kettle, from the kettle to the water, and then from the vapor to the air. Water boils at 100 °C (212 °F).

Celsius (°C)

Fahrenheit (°F)

100

75

50

25

0

200

175

150

125

100

75

50

25

0

Warm It Up!

If heat is a form of energy, where does this energy come from?

Active Reading As you read these two pages, find and underline three facts about friction.

Heat from Friction

You probably already know one way to generate heat. Have you ever rubbed your hands together to keep them warm? When two things rub against each other, friction is produced. Friction changes energy of motion into energy in the form of heat.

There are two ways you can increase the amount of heat you produce. One is to rub your hands faster. The other is to press them together harder as you rub. This is true whenever there is friction. More speed and more pressure mean more energy in the form of heat.

The drill bit is rubbing against the sides of the hole. The bit is moving very quickly, so it produces lots of heat.

Rubbing one piece of wood against another can produce enough heat to start a fire.

Heat from Other Forms of Energy

Energy comes in many different forms. Any of them can be changed into heat energy. The molecules that make up this wood have chemical energy stored in them. When the wood burns, that energy is changed into heat energy.

The space heater below changes electrical energy into heat energy. Heat energy moves from the hot element to the cooler air around it. That makes the air warmer.

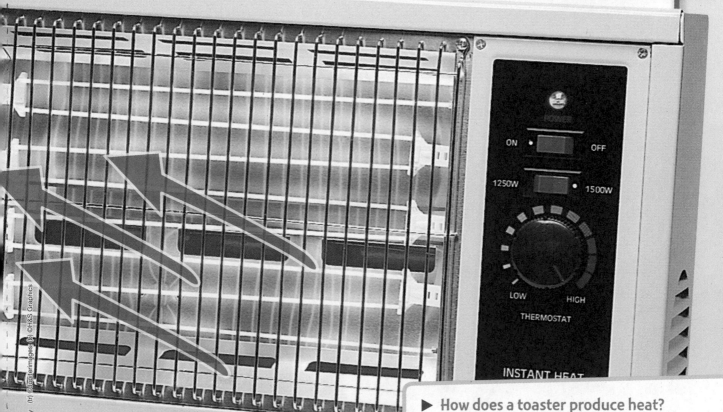

ON OFF

1250W 1500W

LOW HIGH

THERMOSTAT

INSTANT HEAT

▶ How does a toaster produce heat?

_____

_____

Heat on the Move!

Heat energy moves, but how does it get from one place to another?

Active Reading As you read these two pages, draw a box around each main idea.

Heat is conducted from your hand into the snow. The snow melts. Your hand feels cold.

Conduction

Conduction is the transfer, or movement, of heat between two objects that are touching. It can also occur *within* an object. Heat moves from inside your body to warm your skin. Your feet and hands stay warm because heat moves all around your body.

Heat is conducted from the soup to the spoon. Soon the spoon feels hot to the touch.

1. Heat is conducted from the burner to the pot to the water.

2. Heated water travels up, warming the cooler water above.

3. Cooler water sinks to the bottom, where it gets heated. The cycle repeats. This movement is called a *convection current*.

Convection

Convection is the transfer of heat within a liquid or a gas. Particles in liquids and gases move easily, and they take heat with them. Heat from a campfire warms the air around it by convection. Warmer air is always buoyed upward. In this case, the fire is the source of heat for convection.

Hot air is buoyed up above cooler air. That's what keeps a hot-air balloon floating in the air.

▶ Write the kind of heat transfer that takes place in the following situations.

Water warmed by lava on the ocean floor	Winds blowing in from a warmer part of the country	Feet touching a cold floor
_____	_____	_____

Feeling Radiant!

Heat can move through solids, liquids, and gases. But can heat travel without moving through matter? Find out.

Active Reading As you read the next page, draw boxes around the clue words or phrases that signal one thing is being contrasted with another.

Heat travels from the campfire by convection and radiation.

The third way heat can move is radiation. **Radiation** is the transfer of heat without matter to carry it. Heat simply leaves one object and goes directly to another. Suppose you're standing near a campfire. You can feel the heat from the fire because it warms the air. But you can also feel the heat because it warms you directly through radiation.

In some ways, radiation may be the most important way heat can move. Life on Earth needs heat from the sun. But space is a vacuum. How does heat travel through the emptiness of space? By radiation.

The room is cool and air-conditioned. On the other hand, heat radiating from this light keeps the young chickens warm.

► Circle the objects that are radiating heat.

Heat from the sun radiates through space and through the atmosphere before it warms this girl's face.

When you're done, use the answer key to check and revise your work.

Fill in the missing words to complete the conversation.

Summarize

Rebecca: Ow! How did my cell phone get so hot?

Abdullah: Well, there are (1) _____ ways that heat energy could have moved into your phone.

Rebecca: If it had been sitting in sunlight, I'd know it was heated through (2) _____ . But it was in the shade.

Abdullah: Well, there's also convection.

Rebecca: Yeah, but that only happens within (3) _____ and (4) _____ . My phone's a solid.

Abdullah: Then it must have been the third way: (5) _____ .

Rebecca: But that only happens when two things are (6) _____ each other. My phone was sitting by itself.

Abdullah: Where?

Rebecca: On top of my laptop.

Abdullah: In that case, heat traveled into your phone through (7) _____ .

Rebecca: Really? How does it do that?

Abdullah: Heat moves from warm objects to (8) _____ objects. Your laptop was probably much warmer than your cell phone.

Rebecca: Maybe I'll leave it on my wooden desk from now on!

Word Play

1 Unscramble each word and write it in the boxes.

How heat moves from one end of a solid to the other

CCNOTNOIUD

☐ ☐ ☐ ⚪ ⚪ ☐ ☐ ☐

The topic of this lesson

THEA

☐ ⚪ ⚪ ☐

What heat energy does during convection or conduction

SRTFNRAES

☐ ⚪ ☐ ☐ ⚪ ☐ ☐

How heat energy moves through a liquid

TNEVCOINCO

☐ ☐ ☐ ⚪ ☐ ☐ ☐ ☐ ☐

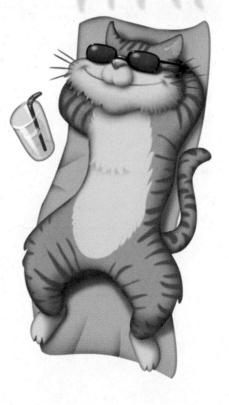

Energy moves from this source by convection and radiation

FIRMPACE

☐ ⚪ ⚪ ☐ ☐ ☐ ☐

How heat energy travels through empty space

DOTAIRNIA

⚪ ☐ ☐ ☐ ⚪ ☐ ☐ ☐

Unscramble the letters in the circles to form a word that is related to this lesson.

_____

Apply Concepts

2 Complete the following statements by filling in the blank.

A. Friction changes energy of _____ into heat energy.

B. When wood burns, _____ energy is changed into heat energy.

C. A space heater turns _____ energy into heat energy.

3 Label each part of the drawing as an example of conduction, convection, or radiation.

A. _____

B. _____

C. _____

© Houghton Mifflin Harcourt Publishing Company

4 Label each of the following as examples of conduction, convection, or radiation.

hot water added to bath

_____

space heater

_____

iron-on decal

_____

clothes dryer

_____

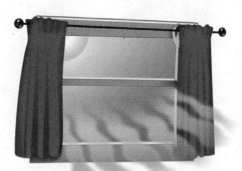

sunlight through a window

_____

sandwich press

_____

5 In this pizza restaurant, heat energy is traveling in different ways. Label the examples of conduction, convection, and radiation in the spaces provided.

Take It Home! With your family, find three devices that give off heat in your home. For each device you find, discuss where the heat comes from and the way in which the heat is transferred.

122

4.1.3 Construct a complete circuit through which an electrical current can pass as evidenced by the lighting of a bulb or ringing of a bell. **4.1.4** Experiment with materials to identify conductors and insulators of heat and electricity. **4.1.5** Demonstrate that electrical energy can be transformed into heat, light, and sound. **Nature of Science**

Name _____

Essential Question

How Can You Identify Conductors and Insulators?

Set a Purpose
What do you think you will learn from this experiment?

_____

_____

State Your Hypothesis
Write your hypothesis, or testable statement.

_____

_____

Think About the Procedure
How will you be able to tell if a material conducts electricity?

_____

_____

How will you be able to tell if a material insulates against heat?

_____

_____

_____

Record Your Data
In the space below, draw a table in which to record your observations.

123

Draw Conclusions

What conclusion can you draw from this investigation?

_____

_____

_____

_____

Do you think paper would be a conductor or an insulator? Explain your answer.

_____

_____

_____

_____

What might be the results if the plastic sheet were thicker?

_____

_____

_____

Analyze and Extend

1. What did most or all of the conductors have in common?

_____

_____

_____

2. What did most or all of the insulators have in common?

_____

_____

_____

3. What other materials do you think might insulate against both electricity and heat?

_____

_____

_____

4. Think of other questions you would like to ask about conductors and insulators.

_____

_____

_____

_____

Name _____

Multiple Choice

4.1.3

1 During planning for an investigation, a student draws four ways she could connect a battery, a paper clip, a light bulb, and some wire. Which arrangement would light the bulb?

Ⓐ

Ⓑ

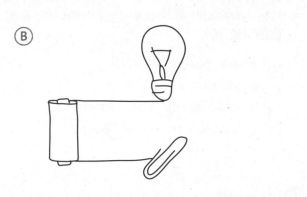

Ⓒ

Ⓓ

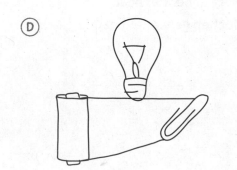

4.1.3

2 What is the purpose of the BATTERY in a simple circuit?

Ⓐ to use the electric current

Ⓑ to connect the components

Ⓒ to provide a source of electrical energy

Ⓓ to change the circuit from open to closed

4.1.5

3 A doorbell circuit includes a source of current, a bell that rings, a button that switches the current on and off, and wires that carry the current. What energy transformation occurs when the doorbell rings?

Ⓐ electrical energy into light energy

Ⓑ electrical energy into sound energy

Ⓒ chemical energy into light energy

Ⓓ mechanical energy into electrical energy

4.1.2

4 Heat energy can move between substances. For example, warm water can warm your hands. Which condition must be present for the transfer of energy between two substances to take place?

Ⓐ The objects must both be solids.

Ⓑ The objects must be the same temperature.

Ⓒ The objects must be different temperatures.

Ⓓ The objects must transfer energy without the use of matter.

4.1.2

5 On a warm sunny day, a lizard sits on a rock. Which statement BEST explains why the lizard feels heat from the sun?

(A) Heat from the sun warms Earth through convection.

(B) Heat from the sun warms Earth through friction.

(C) Heat from the sun warms Earth through gravity.

(D) Heat from the sun warms Earth through radiation.

4.1.4

6 A student needs to choose an item to use as the conductor in a circuit he is making. Which of the following items would be his BEST choice for a conductor of electricity?

(A) metal coin

(B) glass bead

(C) plastic straw

(D) wooden toothpick

4.1.3

7 A student is making a list of reasons the bulb in her circuit does not light. Which of the following COULD BE on her list?

(A) The switch is closed.

(B) The wires make a complete loop.

(C) The light bulb is loose.

(D) The battery is charged.

4.1.2

8 Devon writes a summary of a lesson about heat. Which statement should Devon include in her summary?

(A) Heat always moves from cold objects to warm objects.

(B) Heat is transferred only by conduction.

(C) Heat is a measure of the hotness or coldness of an object.

(D) Heat is the energy transferred between objects of different temperatures.

4.1.2

9 Conduction is one way to transfer heat energy. Which transfer of heat energy demonstrates CONDUCTION?

(A) a hand heats a snowball

(B) a radiator warms a home

(C) a candle warms the air above it

(D) the sun warms a greenhouse

4.1.1

10 When you rub your hands together, you generate heat. Which of the following statements BEST explains this?

(A) Gravity generates heat.

(B) Friction generates heat.

(C) Pressure generates heat.

(D) Conduction generates heat.

4.1.4

11 A student wants to compare how well different materials conduct electricity. He builds a circuit and uses various objects to complete the circuit. He compares how bright a light bulb glows using each object. The table below shows the results.

Object	Glow
nail	very bright
crayon	dim
eraser	very dim
pencil lead	bright

Which object is the BEST conductor of electricity?

Ⓐ The nail is the best conductor.

Ⓑ The crayon is the best conductor.

Ⓒ The eraser is the best conductor.

Ⓓ The pencil lead is the best conductor.

4.1.5

12 In a light bulb, such as the one shown below, the filament glows brightly when the switch is turned on.

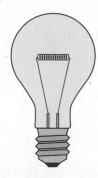

What energy transformation occurs at the filament of a light bulb?

Ⓐ chemical energy into light energy

Ⓑ light energy into electrical energy

Ⓒ kinetic energy into thermal energy and light energy

Ⓓ electrical energy into thermal energy and light energy

4.1.3

13 The electric circuit below consists of a battery, a switch, and three light bulbs.

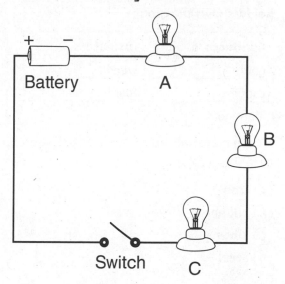

What will happen if the switch is closed and Bulb A is removed?

Ⓐ Bulbs B and C will go out.

Ⓑ Bulb B and C will remain lit.

Ⓒ Bulb B will remain lit and Bulb C will go out.

Ⓓ Bulb C will remain lit and Bulb B will go out.

4.1.1, 4.1.5

14 Energy can transform from one form into another. In which situation is heat generated from another form of energy?

Ⓐ Electrical energy is changed in a toaster.

Ⓑ Sound energy is changed in a microphone.

Ⓒ Kinetic energy is changed in a generator.

Ⓓ Sound energy is changed in a telephone.

4.1.4

15 Carla sorted materials into two groups based on how well they conduct electricity. The table below shows the groups.

Conductors	Insulators
gold	wood
copper	foam
aluminum	

Which material could Carla add to the group of INSULATORS?

- (A) iron
- (B) rubber
- (C) silver
- (D) steel

4.1.4

16 Which of the following definitions BEST describes a conductor of heat?

- (A) a material that produces heat
- (B) a material through which heat can flow easily
- (C) a material through which heat cannot flow easily
- (D) a material that changes heat energy into other forms of energy

4.1.3

17 A student makes an electric circuit that has a switch as one of its parts. The diagram below shows the circuit he makes.

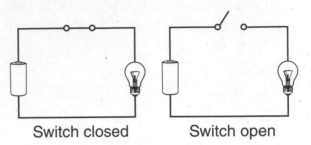

Switch closed   Switch open

What would happen to the light bulb if the student changes the switch from closed to open?

- (A) It would be duller.
- (B) It would be brighter.
- (C) It would stop glowing.
- (D) It would start glowing.

4.1.4

18 Some materials do not conduct electric current. Which of these materials is an electrical INSULATOR?

- (A) a plastic CD case
- (B) a metal paper clip
- (C) a penny
- (D) a staple

4.1.2

19 The statements below describe situations in which heat is transferred from one material to another. In which example is heat transferred through CONVECTION?

- (A) a rock gets warm in the sun
- (B) a spoon gets warm in a bowl of soup
- (C) butter melts on a hot pan
- (D) water comes to a boil in a pot

4.1.1

20 Heat can be generated when two materials rub together. What is the BEST way to increase the amount of heat that is generated?

(A) rub the objects together more quickly and use less pressure

(B) rub the objects together more quickly and use more pressure

(C) rub the objects together more slowly and use less pressure

(D) rub the objects together more slowly and use more pressure

Constructed Response

4.1.2

21 Heat is a form of energy that moves between objects or materials.

Name TWO ways in which heat can be transferred from one object to another.

(1) _____

(2) _____

Describe each type of energy transfer listed above.

(1) _____

(2) _____

4.1.1, 4.1.5

22 Electrical energy can be transformed into other forms of energy. The picture below shows someone using a hair dryer in which electrical energy is changed.

What energy is electrical energy changed into for this appliance to perform its task?

_____

_____

What is another appliance that changes electrical energy into this form of energy?

_____

4.1.3

23 Every day we use items that require electricity. Electric current moves in circuits through these items to power them. To build an electric circuit, we connect different components.

What basic components do all simple closed circuits contain?

_____

_____

Choose one circuit component and describe its role in the circuit.

_____

_____

Extended Response

4.1.3

24 In the electric circuit below, light bulbs are placed at A, B, and C. When the switch is closed, all three light bulbs are lit.

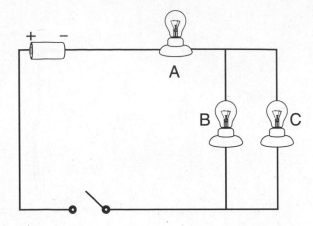

What type of circuit is shown in the diagram?

_____

What will happen to Bulbs A and C if Bulb B burns out?

_____

What will happen to Bulbs B and C if Bulb A burns out?

_____

Describe the purpose and function of the switch in this circuit.

_____

_____

4.1.4

25 A student conducted an experiment to test how well different materials conduct heat energy. She poured an equal amount of warm water into cups made of different materials. Then, she measured the temperature of the water in each cup every five minutes. Her results are shown in the table below.

Material	Temperature (°C)			
	0 min	5 min	10 min	15 min
Plastic-foam	20	20	20	19
Plastic	20	20	19	18
Aluminum	20	18	17	16

Which material is the BEST CONDUCTOR of heat?

_____

Which material is the BEST INSULATOR of heat?

_____

If the student measured the temperature of each cup after 20 minutes, what do you predict would be the temperature of the water in the plastic-foam cup? Explain the reason for your prediction.

_____

What conclusion can you draw from the results shown in the table?

_____

Changes to Earth's Surface

Wabash River, Indiana

I Wonder Where

Water flowing over this standstone has worn amazing patterns in the rock. But where did the rest of the sand go? *Turn the page to find out.*

Here's Where Sand that is washed away from the sandstone flows downstream and is eventually deposited as far away as the Gulf of Mexico.

STANDARD 2
Earth Science

Observe, investigate, and give examples of ways that the shape of the land changes over time. Describe how the supply of natural resources is limited and investigate ways that humans protect and harm the environment.

Essential Question

How Do Weathering and Erosion Shape Earth's Surface?

Engage Your Brain!

Find the answer to the following question in this lesson and record it here.

What could turn a large rock into a giant window?

_____

_____

Active Reading

Lesson Vocabulary

List the terms. As you learn about each one, make notes in the Interactive Glossary.

_____ _____

_____ _____

_____

Cause and Effect

Some ideas in this lesson are connected by a cause-and-effect relationship. Why something happens is a cause. What happens as a result of something else is an effect. Active readers look for effects by asking themselves, What happened? They look for causes by asking why it happened.

133

What can Break a Boulder?

Could a tree root break a rock?
You may think rocks can't break,
but that's not true.

Active Reading As you read these pages, underline all of the different things that can cause a rock to break down.

The process of breaking large rocks into smaller rocks is called **weathering**. Gravity, water, blowing sand, chemicals, and living things, can cause weathering.

Tree roots slowly grow into small cracks in rocks. As roots grow, they become larger. Over time, tree roots can break rocks!

When it rains, water can get into the cracks of rocks.

When water freezes, it expands. This widens the cracks.

Every time water freezes in the cracks of rocks, the cracks become wider. When this happens many times, the rock breaks apart.

Gravity acts on everything. Over time, gravity can cause rocks to fall down a cliff or steep slope and break apart. Temperature changes cause rocks to expand, contract, and eventually to break.

If water gets into a crack in a rock and freezes, when the water expands the rock may break. Flowing water can cause rocks to tumble against each other and break. Water can also wash away rock a little at a time. Similarly, sand blown by wind can scrape against rocks and wear them away.

Living things can also cause weathering. A tree's roots can grow into small cracks in rocks. As the roots grow, they can push the rock apart until it breaks.

Some chemicals in rain can combine with rock and change it so that it crumbles and wears away. Look at the statues on this page. Chemical weathering has already changed one of the statues.

WEATHERED

How will weathering change what this statue looks like?

Draw a picture to show the changes.

Rocks on the Move

Don't rocks just sit around in the sun all day?
No! Rocks can move—find out how.

Weathering is one kind of change that can happen to rocks on Earth's surface. The same wind and water that cause weathering can also carry the broken bits of rock away. The process in which wind, water, ice, or gravity move weathered rock and soil from one place to another is called **erosion** [uh•ROH•zhuhn].

Erosion can be caused by many different natural processes. Moving water is one of the most common causes of erosion. The fast-moving water in this stream can move rocks and soil from the top of the mountain. Together with gravity, water can cause the rocks to move downhill.

The water pulls the pieces of weathered rock and soil along the river's bottom. As the water slows down, it has less energy. It cannot move the largest rocks and pebbles. These are left behind as the water moves on. The dropping of weathered rock by wind or moving water is known as **deposition** [dep•uh•ZISH•uhn].

What happens next?

These pictures show the same part of the Yangtze River before and after a dam was built across the river. How do you think the dam affects the movement of sediment?

_____

_____

_____

BEFORE

AFTER

③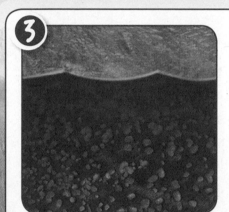

As the water in a river continues to slow down, more bits of weathered rock are dropped. Slow-moving water can carry only very small pieces of rock, such as sand and silt. These bits of rock are called **sediment**.

④

When rivers reach the ocean, they slow down even more. As they slow down, much of the remaining sediment in the water is dropped. Over time, the sediment piles up near the mouth of the river. This makes landforms called *deltas*.

③

Deltas ④

Wind

The wind is just moving air, so what can it do? A lot—wind blows sand and other sediment away.

Wind can carry away soil and other sediment. Strong winds carrying sand can slowly wear away rocks, like the mushroom rock below and the rock arch on the first page of this lesson.

Where does all of it go? Some particles are not carried very far. Others can be carried thousands of miles. Sand from the Sahara Desert, in Africa, is sometimes carried all the way across the Atlantic Ocean to the United States! Wind may deposit a lot of sand in one area, making landforms called *dunes*.

▶ Do you think the mushroom rock shown below formed quickly or slowly? Explain.

_____

_____

_____

_____

_____

_____

This rock, called a mushroom rock, began as a big boulder. Wind slowly eroded the rock, leaving the mushroom shape behind.

EXPOSED BY WIND!

Ice

Can you imagine an ice cube the size of a city? Some chunks of ice are even larger than that!

Active Reading As you read the text, circle two effects glaciers have on Earth's surface.

Huge sheets of ice are called *glaciers*. Glaciers are found in very cold places. You may think that because a glacier is made of ice, it does not move. However, the ice flows like a very slow river. As the glacier flows, it can push rocks as large as boulders.

It also picks up the rock and soil under it, causing erosion. When a glacier begins to melt, the rocks and sediment drop out. The dropped-off sediment forms many different features, including hills called *moraines* [muh•RAYNZ].

A glacier made these grooves in the rock.

CARVED BY ICE!

Glacier Bay, Alaska

Gravity

Gravity is a powerful force! Over time, gravity can bring down a mountain.

Just as gravity causes a ball to fall back to the ground, it causes rocks and sediment to slide down mountains and cliffs. Gravity can even cause huge chunks of rock and soil to slide down a slope all at once. This is called a *landslide*. Landslides happen a lot in mountain ranges. A hill's slope affects how gravity will act on it. If the slope is steep, rocks are much more likely to fall than if the slope is not steep.

BROUGHT DOWN BY GRAVITY!

Do the Math!
Measure Angles

The steepness of a slope is measured in degrees. Use a protractor to measure the three slopes. Record their angles and draw a star next to the steepest slope.

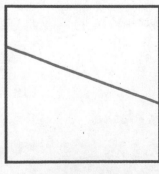

20°

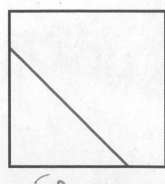

45°

65°

Water

Crashing ocean waves batter the shore with lots of energy! Water can have a dramatic effect on land!

Active Reading As you read the text, circle effects of water erosion.

Flowing water carries sediment down a river. But this is not the only way that water effects the land. Waves crash on rocks along a shore, causing rocks to break apart. The waves cut cliffs and cause caves to form. Waves can also carry away sediment and deposit it in other places. Over time, the constant battering by ocean waves shapes and reshapes the land.

This shape of rock is called a *sea arch*. It forms when waves erode rock, cutting all the way through it.

WASHED AWAY BY WATER!

Carved by Ice

About 20,000 years ago, huge sheets of ice crept over the land. As the ice moved, it slowly carved the land beneath it.

A **glacier** is a huge body of ice and snow that moves over land. In cold places, glaciers form when layers of snow and ice pile up year after year to form giant ice sheets. Gravity causes a glacier to slowly creep downhill.

This huge boulder was carried for miles in frozen glacial ice.

The movement of glaciers created many of the lakes in the Midwest.

During the last ice age, about 20,000 years ago, huge glaciers covered what is now Canada and parts of the United States. During this time, glaciers scraped over the land in the Midwest like giant bulldozers. The moving ice made the land flat in some places, forming plains. In other places, large rolling hills formed.

Glaciers formed other features of the Midwest, too. Rocks, sand, and soil became frozen in the moving ice. When the ice melted, the rocks and soil were dropped off, making the soil rich. Frozen blocks of buried ice melted, forming lakes all over the Midwest. Even the five Great Lakes were carved from glacial ice!

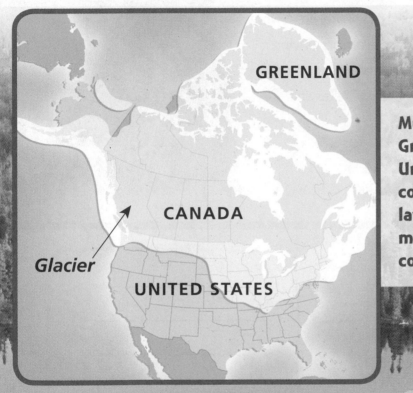

GREENLAND

CANADA

Glacier

UNITED STATES

Much of what is now Canada, Greenland, and parts of the United States were once covered by glaciers. The white layer on the map shows how much of North America was covered with ice!

▶ How do glaciers form? What are the effects of moving glacial ice?

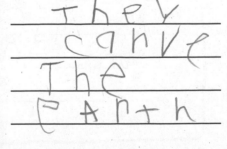

They carve The EArth

143

Sum It Up!

When you're done, use the answer key to check and revise your work.

Use the information in the summary to complete the cause-and-effect graphic organizers.

Summarize

Over time, wind, water, ice, gravity, plants, and animals cause rocks to break down into smaller pieces. Bits of broken-down rock, or sediments, are eroded away by such agents as wind and flowing water. Eventually, the sediments are deposited. Deposited sediments form landforms, such as deltas and sand dunes.

1

Cause	Effect
Water enters the cracks in a rock and freezes into ice.	→ The rock blll cracks

2

Cause	Effect
moving water	→ Sediments are deposited at the mouth of the river and form a delta.

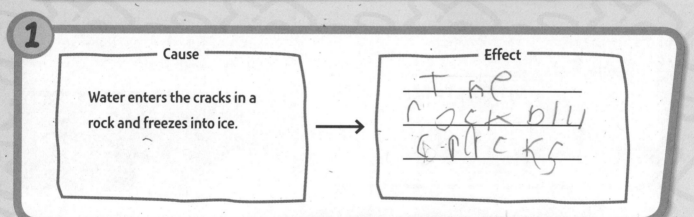

Word Play

1 Read each definition below. Write the letter of the correct word for each definition. Then find and circle the word in the Word Search.

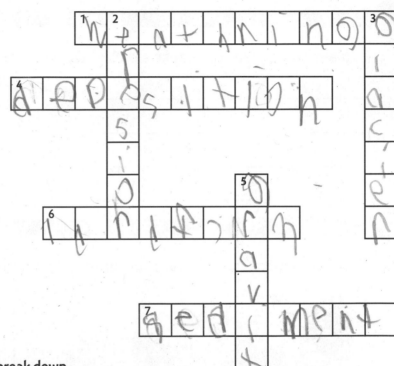

Across

1. What process causes rocks to break down into smaller pieces?

4. What process causes eroded sediments to be dropped off in another place?

6. What is a general name for a feature such as a delta or a sand dune?

7. What are tiny pieces of rock carried by water called?

Down

2. What process carries away weathered rock?

3. What is a large sheet of flowing ice called?

5. What force causes landslides to occur?

| deposition* | erosion* | glacier | gravity |
| landform | sediment* | weathering* | |

*Key Lesson Vocabulary

Apply Concepts

2 Make a list of things that can weather rock.

_____   _____

_____   _____

_____   _____

_____   _____

3 Explain how a plant can cause a rock to weather.

_____

_____

_____

_____

4 Circle the body of water that could erode the largest sediments.

5 For each landform shown, write the word that tells what created the landform. Choose from the list of words below.

wind ice gravity water

_____

_____

_____

6 For each landform below, write whether the landform was formed by erosion or by deposition. Describe how you know your answer is correct.

_____
_____
_____
_____

_____
_____
_____
_____

_____
_____
_____
_____

_____
_____
_____
_____

Take It Home!

With your family, walk through your neighborhood or local park. Find objects that have been left outside for a long time. Describe how you think weathering has changed these objects.

Name _____

4.2.1 Demonstrate and describe how smaller rocks come from the breakage and weathering of larger rocks in a process that occurs over a long period of time.
4.2.2 Demonstrate and describe how wind, water, and glacial ice shape and reshape earth's land surface by eroding rock and soil in some areas and depositing them in other areas in a process that occurs over a long period of time.
Nature of Science

Essential Question

How Do Small Rocks Come from Larger Rocks?

Set a Purpose
What do you think you will learn from this activity?

_____

_____

Think About the Procedure
What natural processes does shaking the jar model?

_____

_____

_____

What natural process does pouring water over the pile of "rocks" model?

_____

_____

Record Your Data
In the space below, draw a before and after picture showing how your "rocks" changed.

149

Draw Conclusions

How did your rock mixture model the weathering of rocks?

_____

_____

_____

Analyze and Extend

1. What changes in the rock mixture did you notice?

_____

_____

2. Did the water in the jar change after you shook the jar? Explain.

_____

_____

_____

3. What happened to the mixture when you poured water over it? What are the names of the two weathering processes that were modeled?

_____

_____

_____

4. What would you expect to happen if you continued to shake the jar?

_____

_____

_____

_____

5. Think of other questions you would like to ask about how rocks are weathered. Write your questions on the lines below.

_____

_____

_____

_____

_____

Essential Question

How Do Earthquakes, Volcanoes, and Landslides Change Earth's Surface?

Engage Your Brain!

Find the answer to the following question in this lesson and record it here.

Did giant gophers tunnel under this city? No. But what could cause this damage?

_____

_____

_____

Active Reading

Lesson Vocabulary

List each term. As you learn about each one, make notes in the Interactive Glossary.

_____

_____

Reading Skill

Some ideas in this lesson are connected by a cause-and-effect relationship. Why something happens is a cause. What happens as a result of something else is an effect. Active readers look for effects by asking themselves what happened. They look for causes by asking why it happened.

Earthquakes

The ground rumbles and shakes. Buildings begin to topple. Roads crack and sink. What is happening?

Active Reading As you read these two pages, draw one line under a cause. Draw two lines under an effect.

Earthquakes happen in just seconds! A sudden shift, or movement of rock below Earth's surface causes an **earthquake**. Most earthquakes happen along a large crack in Earth's crust called a *fault*. The place on Earth's surface directly above the shifting rock is called the *epicenter*. When the rocks shift, waves of vibrations travel out in all directions from the epicenter. The vibrations are strongest at the epicenter and grow weaker as they travel outward.

Most earthquakes are so small that people do not notice them. But some earthquakes are very powerful. They may cause buildings to fall, bridges to crumble, and roads to split, like the one shown here.

Do the Math!
Interpret a Table

The strength of an earthquake is shown using whole numbers and decimals. Higher numbers mean stronger earthquakes.

- Alaska   9.2
- Indiana   5.1
- Maryland 2.6
- California 7.9

Which state in the table had the strongest earthquake? Which state had the weakest earthquake?

The place deep in the earth where an earthquake begins is the focus. Vibrations spread out from the focus to make waves in Earth's surface.

Earthquake Damage

Using an *X*, mark the town where vibrations from the earthquake are strongest. Circle the town that would be least affected by the earthquake.

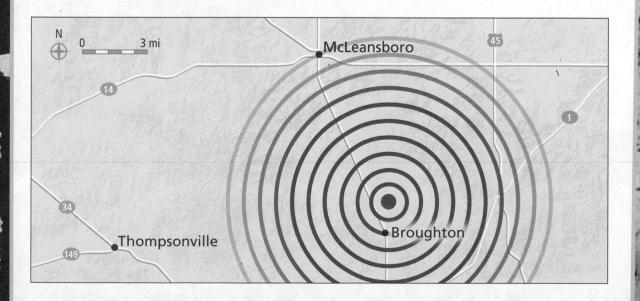

Volcano!

A stream of red-hot melted rock blasts from deep in the Earth. Smoke billows from the top of a mountain. What is going on here?

Active Reading As you read this page, draw a box around the cause and a circle around the effect that is described.

Volcanic eruptions can cause gas, steam, ash, and lava to shoot from the Earth.

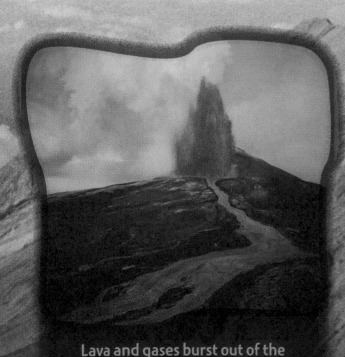

Lava and gases burst out of the top of this volcano.

Lava flows gently down the sides of this volcanic mountain in Hawaii.

volcano is an opening in Earth's crust from which gas, smoke, and melted rock flow. Underneath Earth's surface, high pressure and heat melt rock and produce steam. When layers of rock in the Earth shift, melted rock, called *magma,* may push its way to the surface. When this happens, a volcano erupts.

Once at the surface, the hot melted rock, now called *lava,* flows out of the volcano. As it flows, it begins to cool and harden. This is how volcanic mountains grow.

Some volcanoes erupt with a loud blast! Fountains of lava, gas, and ash may shoot high into the air.

Other times, lava flows quietly and gently downhill.

A Volcano is Born

What causes a volcano to form? Write in the cause or effect.

Cause	Effect
Hot magma reaches Earth's surface.	_____ _____
_____ _____	A volcanic mountain forms and gets bigger.

As lava cools, it hardens into rock. Volcanic rock can be rough and sharp, or smooth like glass.

© Houghton Mifflin Harcourt Publishing Company (bkgd) © G. Sherburne/PhotoLink/Getty Images/PhotoDisc; (b) ©PhotoDisc/Getty Images

Landslide!

A house that was once on top of a hill is now at the bottom. It is partly covered by rocks, soil, and debris! What caused this to happen?

Active Reading As you read these two pages, draw circles around three things that are being compared.

A landslide is the sudden movement of rock and soil down a hill, or slope. Sometimes houses, cars, and trees are carried along. Like earthquakes and volcanoes, a landslide can suddenly change Earth's surface. Landslides can happen anywhere on Earth, even on the ocean floor!

This landslide took place in Los Angeles, California. Like volcanoes and earthquakes, landslides can cause a lot of damage.

Sometimes, an earthquake causes a landslide to happen.

The vibrations shake rocks and other materials on a slope. Gravity does the rest of the work by pulling the loose materials quickly down a slope.

At times, heavy rains may soak the soil on a slope. Gravity then acts on the very wet soil, and down comes a river of mud, rock, trees, and even houses! This movement of land is called a *mudslide*.

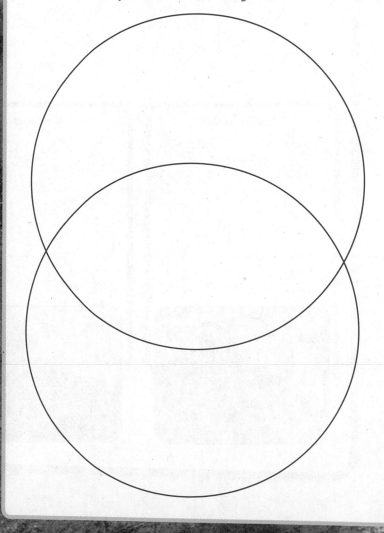

Comparing Landslides

Compare and contrast a landslide with a volcano. Complete the Venn diagram.

Sum It Up!

When you're done, use the answer key to check and revise your work.

Read the summary. Write each number from the list below in the correct box at the bottom of the page.

Summarize

Many natural events can change Earth's surface. Earthquakes, volcanoes, and landslides are some examples. Sometimes, the events cause little or no change to the land. Other times, the changes they cause are enormous and very sudden.

1. magma
2. rocks and soil
3. waves of vibrations
4. epicenter
5. lava

6. heavy rain
7. fault line
8. gravity
9. erupt
10. Add your own detail to one box below.

Earthquake	Volcano	Landslide/Mudslide

Brain Check

Name _____

Word Play

1 Read each definition below. Write the letter of the correct word for each definition. Then find and circle the word in the Word Search.

Red-hot melted rock deep inside Earth _____

A large crack in the rock layers of Earth's crust _____

A sudden movement of rocks and soil down a slope _____

Hot, melted rock that reaches Earth's surface _____

A sudden shift or movement of rock layers below Earth's surface _____

An opening in Earth's crust from which melted rock flows _____

The place on Earth just above where an earthquake occurs _____

a	g	t	h	f	j	d	k	w	o	x	m	o	l	k	m	t
m	b	a	f	n	p	t	c	l	l	o	p	a	o	x	g	s
c	y	e	a	r	t	h	q	u	a	k	e	e	g	i	s	d
v	c	b	u	o	t	i	a	e	n	n	p	n	s	m	d	d
d	v	o	l	c	a	n	o	r	d	s	b	e	p	a	a	k
w	m	a	t	h	c	r	p	o	s	h	c	s	o	d	o	n
b	v	a	e	r	l	s	o	p	l	u	f	w	l	o	q	j
i	l	a	b	a	a	s	e	p	i	c	e	n	t	e	r	b
y	d	r	l	i	v	a	r	m	d	r	i	d	a	c	d	y
x	l	e	r	c	a	t	s	h	e	b	r	r	s	t	a	e

A. volcano*	B. landslide*	C. magma	D. epicenter
E. fault	F. lava	G. earthquake*	

Apply Concepts

2 Choose one natural event that you read about. Draw a picture of the land before the event happened. Then, draw a picture to show the land after the event happened. Describe your pictures.

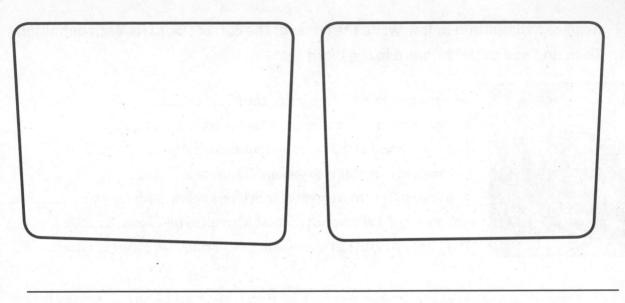

_____

_____

_____

3 Fill in the flow chart to show the sequence of events that lead to a volcanic eruption.

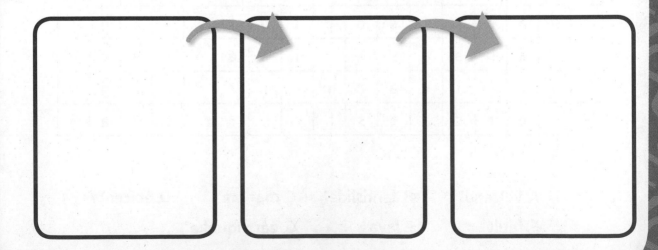

4 Imagine you are a house on a hill. A landslide occurs on your hill. Describe what caused the landslide and what happens from the point of view of the house.

_____

_____

_____

_____

_____

5 Look at the picture below. Choose a spot where an earthquake happens. Which of the towns on the map will feel the earthquake most? Explain why.

_____

_____

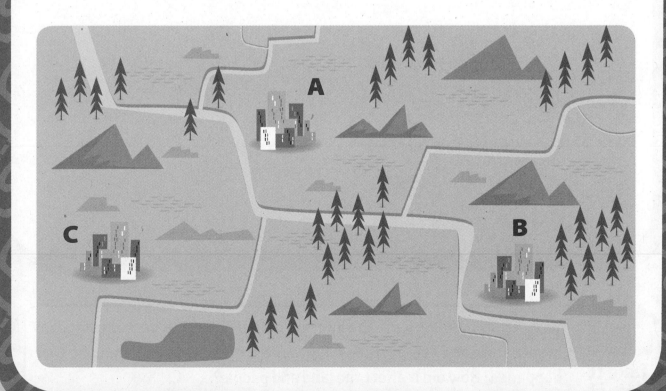

6 Imagine you are taking a trip below Earth's surface near a volcano. Describe what you might see.

_____

_____

_____

7 Describe how earthquakes, volcanoes, and landslides are alike and how they are different. Then draw a Venn diagram to represent your description.

_____

_____

_____

_____

Take It Home!

With family members, use the Internet to find out about past earthquakes in your state or a nearby state. What was the most severe earthquake that happened? How did it affect the land and people?

Ask a Volcanologist

Q. What does a volcanologist do?

A. A volcanologist is a person who studies volcanoes. We can warn people when a volcano will erupt. People will have time to get to safety.

Q. How do you stay safe when working around lava?

A. I wear special clothes, gloves, and boots to protect me from the heat. I wear a gas mask to protect me from volcanic gases.

Q. How do you know that lava is very hot?

A. Lava is very hot! You know that lava is hot because it gives off heat and light. It may glow bright orange, yellow, or red.

Now It's Your Turn!

▶ What question would you ask a volcanologist?

_____

_____

_____

_____

Be a Volcanologist

Volcanologists can tell lava's temperature by the color it glows.

Match each temperature below to the lava flowing from the volcano. Write the temperature in the correct location.

1100°C	bright orange
850°C	bright red
650°C	dark red
200°C	black

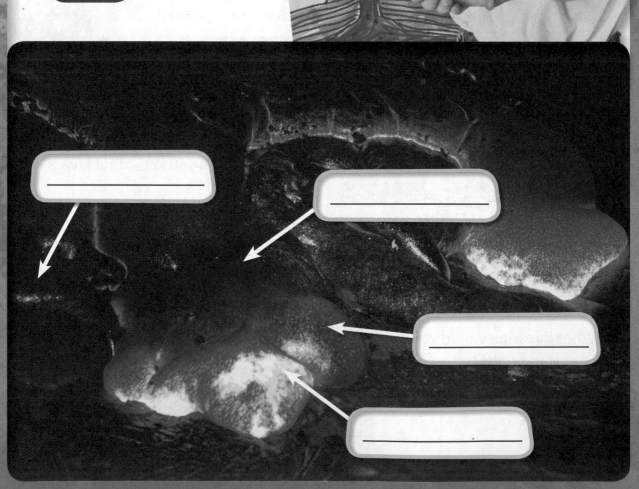

4.2.3 Demonstrate and describe how earthquakes, volcanoes, and landslides suddenly change the shape of the land.
Nature of Science

Name _____

Essential Question

How Can You Model Sudden Changes to the Land?

Set a Purpose
What do you think you will learn from this activity?

_____

_____

_____

_____

Think About the Procedure
Why do you think you are building your model inside a cardboard box top? Explain.

_____

_____

_____

_____

Record Your Data
In the space below, write what you predict will happen, then draw what you observe.

Draw Conclusions

Did your model successfully show how the land changes after a volcano? Explain.

_____

_____

_____

_____

Analyze and Extend

1. Compare and contrast your model with the real event. How does your model help you understand what happens?

_____

_____

_____

2. Compare and contrast your model with another group. How are the models alike? How do they differ?

_____

_____

_____

_____

3. What changes could you make to improve your model? Explain why you would make these changes.

_____

_____

_____

_____

4. Think of other questions you would like to ask about how natural events change the land. Write your questions on the lines below.

_____

_____

Essential Question

How Can We Use Resources Wisely?

Engage Your Brain!

Find the answer to the following question in this lesson and record it here.

What resource is being used and what resource is being produced?

_____

_____

Active Reading

Lesson Vocabulary

List each term. As you learn about each one, make notes in the Interactive Glossary.

_____

_____

_____

Reading Skill

Signal words show connections between ideas. *For example* and *for instance* signal example of an idea. *Also* and *in fact* signal added facts. Active readers remember what they read because they are alert to signal words that show examples and facts about a topic.

Natural Resources

Are you wearing jeans? Do you write on paper? Where do all the things we use come from?

Active Reading As you read these two pages, circle clue words that signal a detail such as an example or added fact.

Each day, you use natural **resources**—materials found in nature that are used by living things. All of the things that people use begin as some form of natural resource.

Some resources, like fresh water and clean air are both renewable and not renewable. How is this possible? If air and water stay clean, they can be used again and again. But air and water can be polluted. **Pollution** is any harmful substance in the environment. Pollution is difficult to remove. So in that way, clean air and clean water can also be non-renewable.

Stone used in buildings, tunnels, and bridges are mined from stone quarries. It takes millions of years and the right conditions to make stone.

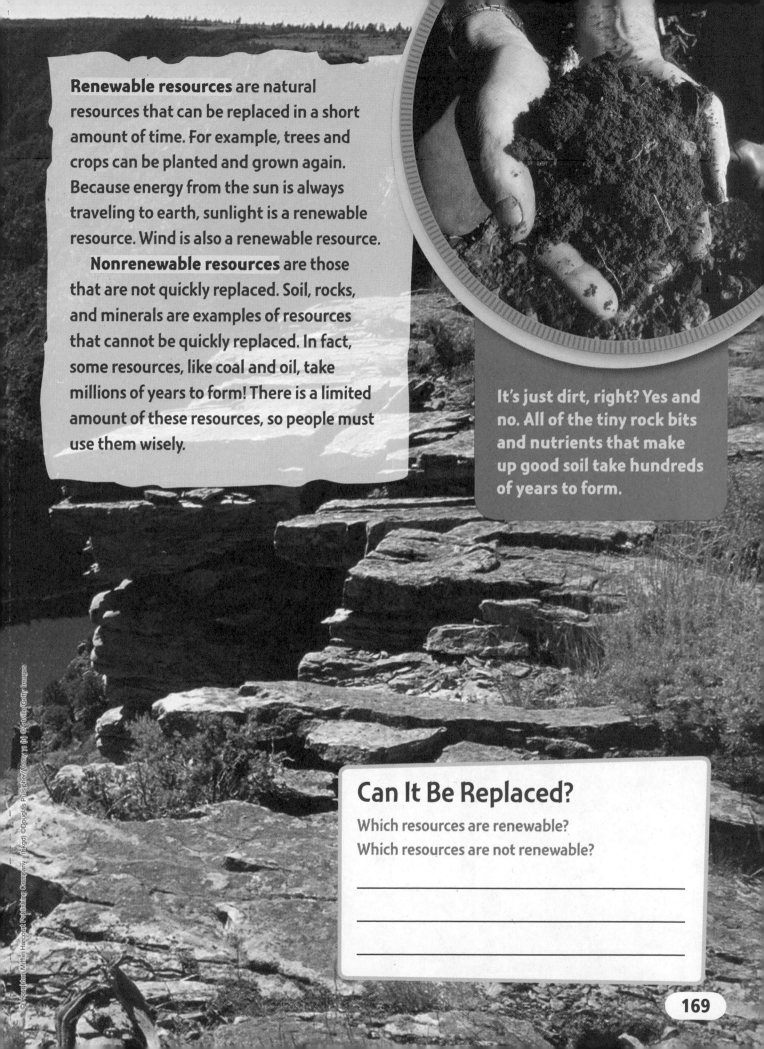

Renewable resources are natural resources that can be replaced in a short amount of time. For example, trees and crops can be planted and grown again. Because energy from the sun is always traveling to earth, sunlight is a renewable resource. Wind is also a renewable resource.

Nonrenewable resources are those that are not quickly replaced. Soil, rocks, and minerals are examples of resources that cannot be quickly replaced. In fact, some resources, like coal and oil, take millions of years to form! There is a limited amount of these resources, so people must use them wisely.

It's just dirt, right? Yes and no. All of the tiny rock bits and nutrients that make up good soil take hundreds of years to form.

Can It Be Replaced?

Which resources are renewable?
Which resources are not renewable?

_____

_____

_____

Fossil Fuels

Energy from the sun is stored in the bodies of living things. What happens when this energy is buried?

Millions of years ago, the remains of ancient organisms became buried in the Earth. Energy was stored in these buried plants and animals. Over time, heat and pressure in the Earth changed the plant and animal remains. Some became rocks we call fossils. Others became **fossil fuels**, an energy source formed from the remains of dead organisms. Fossil fuels include coal, oil, and natural gas.

When fossil fuels are burned, stored energy is released, or given off. These natural energy resources are used to power cars, heat homes, and make electricity.

Because it takes millions of years for fossil fuels to form, they are nonrenewable resources. There are limited amounts of fossil fuels. They cannot be replaced.

The burning of fossil fuels produces a lot of useful energy, but it also causes pollution of air and water.

© Houghton Mifflin Harcourt Publishing Company (bkgd) ©Corbis

▶ Make a list of ways you can use less fossil fuels.

_____

_____

Oil is found deep inside the Earth. Oil rigs have special drills that can reach the oil and then pump it to the surface for people to use.

Coal mines are deep inside the Earth. Miners must bring coal to the surface.

Save It!

If people protect Earth's natural resources and use them wisely, they will last longer. Our resources must last us well into the future!

People use more and more energy to power all the things we use at school, work, and home. Most of this energy is produced by burning fossil fuels. To keep fossil fuels from being used up, people must cut back on their use. **Conservation** is the wise use of natural resources. When we conserve natural resources, we help them to last longer.

Using less electricity means using less coal, so Earth's coal supplies will be extended or last longer.

Some ways of farming, like the terraced farming shown here, help to keep soil from being washed away.

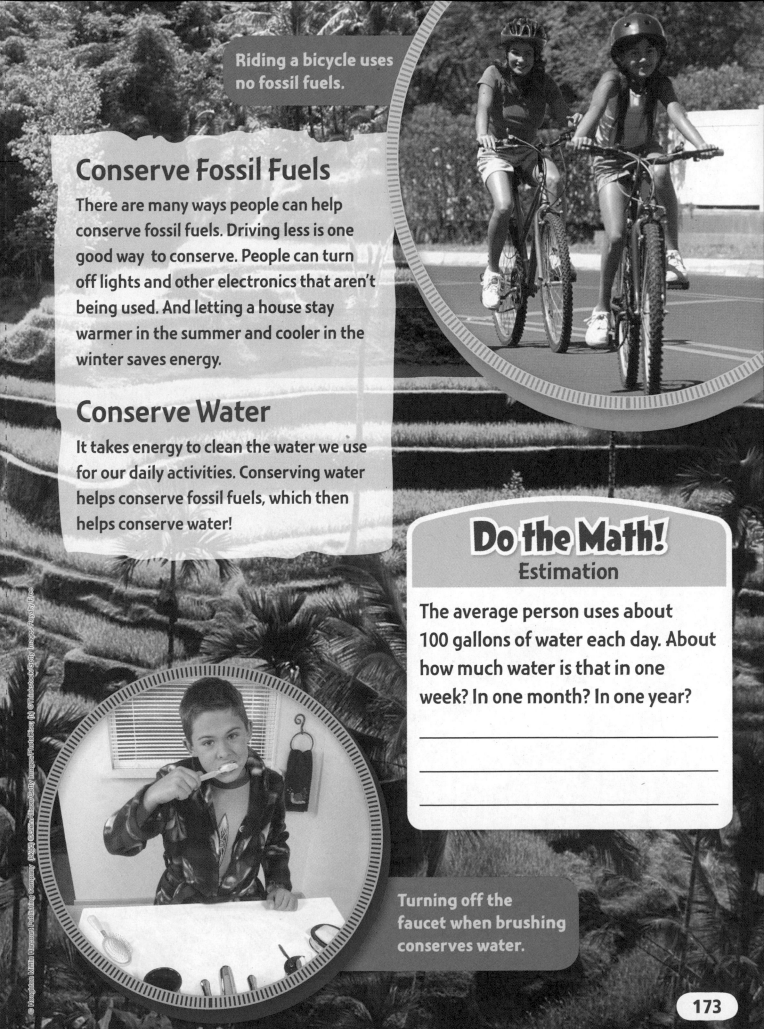

Riding a bicycle uses no fossil fuels.

Conserve Fossil Fuels

There are many ways people can help conserve fossil fuels. Driving less is one good way to conserve. People can turn off lights and other electronics that aren't being used. And letting a house stay warmer in the summer and cooler in the winter saves energy.

Conserve Water

It takes energy to clean the water we use for our daily activities. Conserving water helps conserve fossil fuels, which then helps conserve water!

Do the Math!
Estimation

The average person uses about 100 gallons of water each day. About how much water is that in one week? In one month? In one year?

_____

_____

_____

Turning off the faucet when brushing conserves water.

Let's Recycle ♻

Where do used bottles, cans, and newspapers go? Often they end up in a landfill, but they can be used over and over again!

Active Reading As you read these two pages, write numbers next to the pictures to show the steps of glass recycling.

People put glass into recycling bins.

The glass is shipped to a recycling company.

At the recycling center, the glass is sorted by color.

One way to conserve resources is to **recycle**, or use materials over again. Glass bottles, metal cans, plastic, and paper are made from resources such as sand, aluminum, oil, and wood. When we recycle glass, metal, plastic, and paper, we conserve the resources they came from. We also have less trash.

You might be surprised at the things in your home that are made from recycled materials. Paper is made into new products such as cereal boxes, pencils, or calendars. You may even be wearing a t-shirt made from recycled plastic!

Reuse It!

What are some ways that you could reuse a glass bottle or jar?

The glass is crushed into tiny pieces, then cleaned and dried.

The crushed glass is melted and then blown into new bottles and jars.

Sum It Up!

When you're done, use the answer key to check and revise your work.

Read the summary. Write each number from the list below in the correct box at the bottom of the page.

Summarize

People use Earth's resources to meet their needs. Some resources are renewable. They can be replaced in a short amount of time. Other resources are nonrenewable. There are limited supplies of nonrenewable resources because they can take hundreds, thousands, or even millions of years to replace!

1. coal

2. plants

3. trees

4. natural gas

5. wind

6. oil

7. soil

8. minerals

9. sunlight

10. rocks

Renewable Resources

Nonrenewable Resources

Word Play

1 Use the words in the box to complete the puzzle.

Across

1. a renewable energy source
2. a resource that is not easily replaced
3. water is an example of this kind of resource
4. a way of using glass, paper, plastic, and metal over again

Down

5. the act of using resources wisely
6. a nonrenewable resource deep in Earth
7. resources formed from remains of ancient organisms
8. a resource used to make electricity

| *renewable | coal | *conservation | *fossil fuel |
| sunlight | *nonrenewable | oil | *recycle |

*Key Lesson Vocabulary

Apply Concepts

2 Draw a picture of a renewable resource. Then draw a picture of one way to conserve this resource. Label your pictures.

Renewable Resource

One Way to Conserve

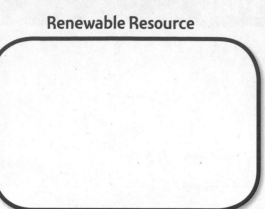

3 Fill in the flow chart to show the sequence of steps that happen when glass is recycled.

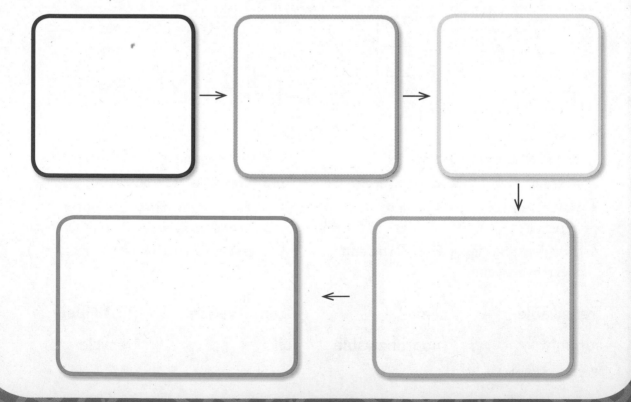

4 List two nonrenewable resources you read about. Draw a picture of how people might use each of these resources.

_____   _____

5 Make a list of things that can be recycled. Choose one. Draw or describe one way you could reuse it.

_____

_____

_____

_____

_____

6 Match each resource in the box to the picture that shows how people use the resource. Next to each resource in the box write an *R* for renewable or an *N* for nonrenewable.

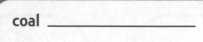

coal _____

oil _____

trees_____

soil _____

water_____

rocks_____

Explain why one of these resources can be considered both renewable and nonrenewable.

_____

Take It Home! With a family member, make a list of things in your home that come from recycled materials.

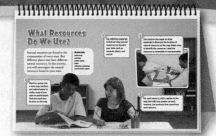

4.2.4 Investigate earth materials that serve as natural resources and gather data to determine which are in limited supply.
Nature of Science

Name _____

Essential Question

What Resources Do We Use?

Set a Purpose
What do you think you will learn from this activity?

_____

_____

_____

Think About the Procedure
What reference materials will you use to find out about resources in your state?

_____

_____

Record Your Data
In the space below, make a table to list resources and where they're found.

Draw Conclusions

Which natural resources are there the most of in your state?

_____

_____

_____

Analyze and Extend

1. What do you notice about where natural resources are found in your state?

_____

_____

_____

2. Make a table below that lists each resource on your map and one way that people use the resource.

```
┌─────────────────────────────┐
│                             │
│                             │
│                             │
│                             │
│                             │
│                             │
│                             │
│                             │
└─────────────────────────────┘
```

3. With your group, choose one of the resources. Design an investigation to find out how much of this resource is available in your state now. Then find out how much of this resource is likely to be available 100 years from now.

_____

_____

_____

4. Based on your map, which resource in your state do you think is the most important to conserve?

_____

_____

_____

5. Think of other questions you would like to ask about the resources you use. Write your questions on the lines below.

_____

_____

_____

_____

Name _____

Multiple Choice

4.2.1

1 Joshua spends the day at the beach with his family. He finds some smooth stones in the sand. What process causes the stones to become smooth?

(A) erosion by waves

(B) glacial grooving

(C) weathering by motion

(D) deposition of the stones

4.2.2

2 Notice the size of the rocks in the image below.

Which process could cause a large pile of rocks of this size to be found in the same place?

(A) deposition by rainwater

(B) polishing from plant materials

(C) weathering by water and wind

(D) erosion caused by running water

4.2.1, 4.2.2

3 Wind, water, and ice are involved in both weathering and erosion. However, weathering and erosion are two different processes. Which sentence states a DIFFERENCE between weathering and erosion?

(A) Erosion moves rocks to a new location.

(B) Weathering moves rocks from place to place.

(C) Erosion breaks down rocks but does not move them.

(D) Weathering moves rocks without breaking them down.

4.2.2

4 A sand spit is a landform found along a coastline. The spit connects to the mainland at one end. The other end juts into open water. Which statement is TRUE about how sand spits are formed?

(A) Sea animals move sand to form sand spits.

(B) Sand spits are found only in warm climates.

(C) Sand spits are built by humans as mainland extensions.

(D) Ocean waves and currents deposit sand to form sand spits.

4.2.2

5 A glacier is a large mass of slow-moving ice that flows down a slope. Glaciers cause erosion on Earth. Which of the following landforms is created by a glacier?

(A) sand spit

(B) moraine

(C) dust bowl

(D) barrier island

4.2.2

6 The action created by wind, water, or ice may have the effect of leaving a solid material behind. Which of the following descriptions is an example of deposition?

Ⓐ a steep canyon

Ⓑ sand in a river delta

Ⓒ a large hole in a cliff wall

Ⓓ a crack in a boulder after winter

4.2.2

7 Alluvial fans are fan-shaped deposits of sediment that are created by the flow of water.

Where is an alluvial fan MOST LIKELY to form?

Ⓐ at the tip of a glacier

Ⓑ at the edge of a canyon

Ⓒ at the top of a mountain

Ⓓ at the bottom of a steep slope

4.2.2

8 The flow of water can cause soil erosion. This diagram shows soil erosion caused by rain.

If the homeowner wants to stop the process of erosion, what can he or she do?

Ⓐ Plant grass.

Ⓑ Install a sprinkler.

Ⓒ Fill the hole with dirt.

Ⓓ Pile the dirt back up on the slope.

4.2.1

9 Weathering is defined as the process by which rocks are broken down into smaller pieces. Which of the following choices is an example of weathering?

Ⓐ glaciers creating moraines

Ⓑ plant roots breaking apart rock

Ⓒ wind blowing dust across flat land

Ⓓ ocean waves depositing sand on beaches

4.2.2

10 Glaciers cause weathering as they move down a slope. What is one effect of such weathering?

Ⓐ sinkholes
Ⓑ moraines
Ⓒ sand spits
Ⓓ glacial grooves

4.2.3

11 Some natural events cause landforms to change quickly. Other events cause change slowly. Which of the following events will MOST LIKELY cause landforms to change quickly?

Ⓐ erosion
Ⓑ glacier
Ⓒ earthquake
Ⓓ weathering

4.2.2

12 Sand dunes are the result of a natural process.

What will MOST LIKELY cause a sand dune to form?

Ⓐ eroding of alluvial fans
Ⓑ weathering of rocks and shells
Ⓒ wind blowing sand against beach grass
Ⓓ storms washing sand away from the beach

4.2.2

13 A moraine is a ridge of deposited rock and sediment. What causes a moraine to form?

Ⓐ glacier
Ⓑ sinkhole
Ⓒ landslide
Ⓓ sand dune

4.2.2

14 Although natural elements cause erosion, they can also help stop erosion. Which of the following items BEST helps reduce soil erosion?

Ⓐ plants
Ⓑ sunshine
Ⓒ strong wind
Ⓓ running water

4.2.1

15 Weathering is the process by which rocks are broken down into smaller pieces. Which of the following can break a rock apart?

Ⓐ barrier island
Ⓑ plant roots
Ⓒ sand dune
Ⓓ sand spit

4.2.4

16 The picture below shows a forest.

Which states the BEST reason why trees are considered a renewable resource?

Ⓐ Trees can be burned as a fuel.

Ⓑ It takes many years for a tree to reach its full height.

Ⓒ New trees will grow to replace trees that are cut down.

Ⓓ The trees will eventually form fuels, such as oil and coal.

4.2.2, 4.2.4

17 Marc's family owns a farm. Last year, when they were clearing the fields, he noticed that the wind blew a lot of the soil away. Which of the following would be MOST helpful to reduce the loss of soil?

Ⓐ Bring in sand from a beach.

Ⓑ Plant trees around the fields.

Ⓒ Water down the fields each day.

Ⓓ Plant grass seed with their crops.

4.2.2, 4.2.4

18 A new mall is being built near Min's house. One day, she notices that the construction equipment has cleared away all the trees and grass on a hillside. The next day, a rainstorm washes away a lot of the soil. What would BEST prevent this from happening again?

Ⓐ Clear the grass below the hill.

Ⓑ Cover the hillside with sand.

Ⓒ Remove soil from the hillside.

Ⓓ Plant new grass on the hillside.

4.2.3

19 The figure shows an earthquake.

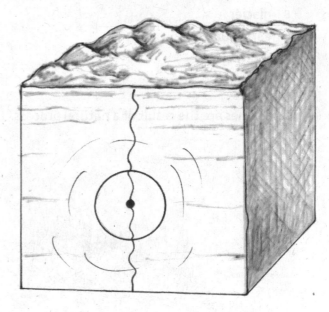

What is represented by the dot inside the circle?

Ⓐ uplift

Ⓑ a fault line

Ⓒ the focus

Ⓓ seismic waves

4.2.3

20 The picture shows where a landslide occurred.

Which is MOST LIKELY to cause a landslide?

(A) gravity and excess rain

(B) formation of mud and rocks

(C) planting ground cover and boulders

(D) running water and sandy soil that drains well

Constructed Response

4.2.1, 4.2.2

21 Erosion and weathering both affect earth materials, but they can affect them in different ways.

Explain how erosion and weathering are similar.

_____

_____

Explain how erosion is different from weathering.

_____

_____

4.2.4

22 Some resources are renewable, and some resources are nonrenewable.

What is the difference between a renewable resource and a nonrenewable resource?

_____

_____

List two examples of each type of resource, and explain why it is renewable or nonrenewable.

_____

_____

4.2.3

23 Earthquakes occur when forces push Earth along a fault line.

What major, rapid changes occur in Earth during an earthquake?

_____

_____

Describe two examples of damage to property caused by earthquakes.

_____

_____

Extended Response

4.2.1, 4.2.2, 4.2.3

24 Forces in nature cause landforms to change both slowly and quickly.

Describe how erosion can cause landforms to change quickly.

_____

_____

How can erosion cause landforms to change slowly?

_____

_____

Explain how weathering causes landforms to change slowly.

_____

_____

Describe at least two other ways landforms can change quickly.

_____

_____

4.2.4

25 The following diagram shows what happens when aluminum is recycled.

At the recycling center, the cans are either shredded into small pieces, or they are compressed into large blocks.

Aluminum cans are brought to the recycling center.

The pieces or blocks are shipped to a processing plant.

The flat aluminum sheets are used to make cans.

At the plant, the pieces or blocks are melted in a furnace. Any labels or coatings on the cans are burned off.

The hot, liquid aluminum is cooled into blocks. Before the blocks are all the way cool, the aluminum is rolled out into flat sheets.

Which step comes first in the process?

_____

_____

What happens to aluminum cans at the recycling center?

_____

_____

Describe what happens to aluminum at the processing plant.

_____

_____

Why is this process in the shape of a circle?

_____

_____

Adaptations and Survival

Hoary bat

I Wonder Why

Why does this bat have large, wrinkly ears?
Turn the page to find out.

Here's Why Living things, like this bat, have characteristics that help them survive in their environment. The bat's wrinkly ears help funnel sound waves so that the bat can use echoes to fly in the dark!

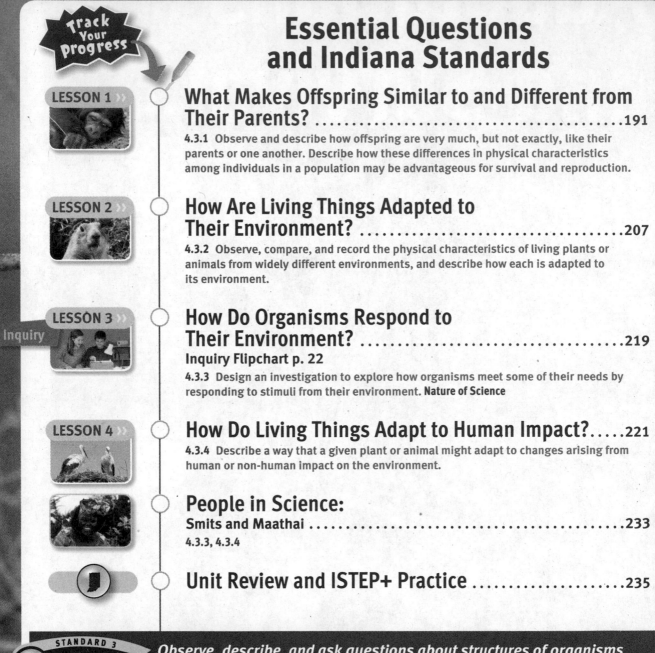

Track Your Progress

Essential Questions and Indiana Standards

STANDARD 3
Life Science

Observe, describe, and ask questions about structures of organisms and how they affect their growth and survival.

Essential Question

What Makes Offspring Similar to and Different from Their Parents?

Engage Your Brain!

Find the answer to the following question in this lesson and record it here.

Why is this young zebra similar to, but not the same as, its mother?

_____

_____

_____

_____

Active Reading

Lesson Vocabulary

List the terms. As you learn about each one, make notes in the Interactive Glossary.

_____

_____

_____

_____

Main Idea

The main idea of a paragraph is the most important idea. The main idea may be stated in the first sentence, or it may be stated elsewhere. Active readers look for main ideas by asking themselves "What is this paragraph mostly about?"

Like Mother, Like Child

Have you ever noticed how children often look a lot like their parents? This happens because of a process known as heredity.

Active Reading As you read these two pages, circle the inherited traits.

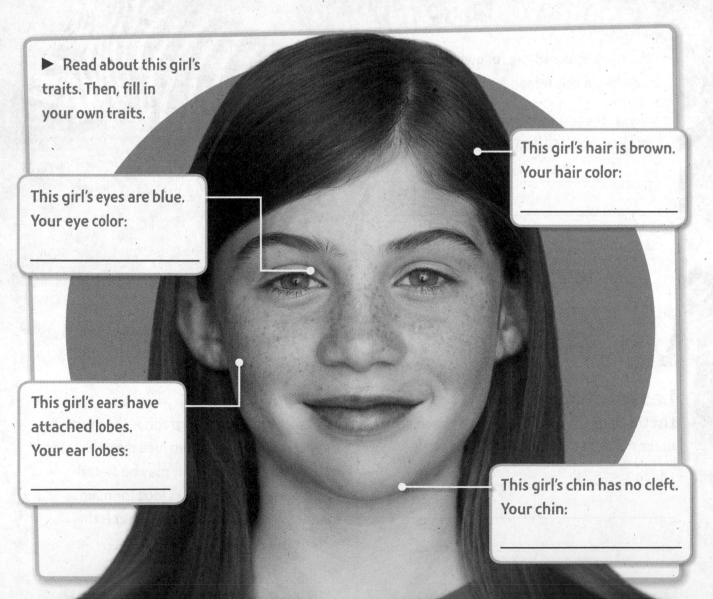

▶ Read about this girl's traits. Then, fill in your own traits.

This girl's hair is brown.
Your hair color:
_____

This girl's eyes are blue.
Your eye color:
_____

This girl's ears have attached lobes.
Your ear lobes:
_____

This girl's chin has no cleft.
Your chin:
_____

Snapdragon Family Tree

Traits, such as flower color, are passed down from one generation to the next. Tracking a trait makes a branching diagram called a family tree.

The passing of traits from parents to offspring is **heredity**. A *trait* is a feature of an individual, such as brown eyes.

All of the features you see when you look in the mirror are traits. Most of these traits came from your parents. For example, suppose you have a friend with blue eyes. Most likely, one or both of your friend's parents also have blue eyes. Your friend inherited his eye color from his parents.

Heredity happens in other living things as well. As you can see on this page, flowers inherit their petal color from their parents. Birds inherit their beak shape. And giraffes inherit their long necks. This is why family members look similar to one other.

It's in the Genes

Every living thing contains chemical instructions for traits. These instructions are called genes.

Active Reading Underline the main idea as you read each paragraph below.

Half of your genes came from your mother. The other half came from your father. Because of this, you have a mixture of traits from both of your parents.

Remember that a sperm is a male sex cell. It contains genes from the father. An egg is a female sex cell. It has genes from the mother. When the two sex cells join, the resulting cell has genes from both parents.

Genes [JEENZ] are instructions for traits. These instructions are carried on X-shaped chemicals. This chicken got half its genes from its mother, and half from its father.

▶ What might be a benefit of making plants resistant to poison? What might be a problem with this genetic change?

Benefits	Problems

The genes of some of these carrots have been changed so the carrots are different colors.

Genetic Engineering

Scientists have learned a lot about how genes control traits. Today, scientists can take genes from one living thing and put them in another. This is called genetic engineering. Scientists use genetic engineering to change a living thing's traits. For example, they can make carrots more nutritious by adding genes for different vitamins. They can make plants that aren't killed by poisons. They can make bacteria that produce medicines. Because this technology is fairly new, the effects are still being studied.

Mom?! Why are my carrots **maroon?**

Genes + Environment = You

Your genes alone do not control all of your traits. The environment you live in affects your traits, too!

Active Reading As you read this page and the next one, put a star next to a main idea, and circle a supporting detail.

Skin color can be changed by the environment. Staying in the sun can make your skin darker. Too much sun is dangerous. Be sure to always wear sunblock.

The flower color of this hydrangea [hy•DRAYN•juh] is affected by the soil. Sometimes, the flowers are pink. If the soil becomes acidic, the flowers turn blue.

Some traits are caused when your genes and environment interact. For example, your height is controlled by genes. But it also is controlled by the kinds of foods you eat. If you did not eat nutritious food, you would not grow as tall as you could on a healthy diet.

Can you think of other traits you have that are affected by the environment?

Like you, other living things have traits caused by a mix of genes and other factors. For example, plants grow towards light.

If you leave a houseplant near a window, it will grow towards the window. No matter where you move the plant, it will start to grow towards the strongest light.

The environment can change living things in other ways, as well. For example, a tadpole is a frog larva that swims in water. If the pond tadpoles live in starts to dry up, they will undergo metamorphosis at a faster rate. They will become adult frogs faster than tadpoles left in deep ponds.

Do the Math!
Make a Number Line

The sex of alligators is affected by temperature. Alligator eggs that develop at 30 °C or less will all be female. Eggs that develop at 34 °C or more will all be male. Eggs that develop at temperatures between 30 °C and 34 °C will have some male and some female alligators. Use this information to label the temperature line below.

```
|----|----|----|----|----|----|----|----|----|----|
0    5   10   15   20   25   30   35   40   45   50
```

Living Things Change

Each of these corn snakes looks a little different. Sometimes, little differences can make a big difference in survival!

Corn snakes live in a wide variety of habitats in the United States. In the wild, corn snakes come in several different colors.

Active Reading As you read these pages, circle the two clue words that signal a detail about a main idea.

You have learned that offspring are different from their parents. Every organism is slightly different from every other organism. Sometimes these differences can be very important.

Corn snakes, like the ones shown here, come in many colors and patterns. Some are very light colored, some are golden brown, and some are bright orange. Suppose a hawk is flying over a light golden wheat field, looking for a snack. Which of these snakes is least likely to become lunch?

If you guessed the golden brown snake, you are correct. Why? Its color would blend in with the wheat. The hawk would not see it, and the snake would survive. The snake would reproduce and pass on its coloring to its offspring. Its golden brown offspring would have a better chance of surviving in the wheat field and would also produce more offspring. Eventually, most of the snakes living in the wheat field would be golden brown.

Sometimes living things change because their environment changes. For example, bacteria have changed as a result of their changing environment. Since the discovery of antibiotics, people have learned how to kill bacteria. But in a very large population of bacteria, a few are not affected by penicillin. These bacteria survive and multiply. Over time, they produce large populations of bacteria that are not affected by penicillin.

Antibiotics in soaps and cleaners kill many bacteria. However, when not all of the bacteria are killed, the ones that survive multiply. Little by little, bacteria are becoming resistant to antibacterial soap and cleaners.

Blending In

Which of the three snakes shown would be most likely to survive in a forest?

_____

_____

_____

_____

There are many products that kill bacteria. Over time, bacteria will not be killed by these products and new products will have to be developed.

Sanitizing **Antibacterial** Kitchen Wipes

Antibacterial Soap

Antibacterial Ointment

Insight into Instincts

Not all behaviors are learned. Animals are born knowing how to do some kinds of things.

Active Reading As you read the text below, draw a circle around all the examples of instinctive behaviors.

Behaviors that an animal is born knowing how to do are called **instincts.** Like physical traits, animals inherit their instincts from their parents. Birds build nests because of instincts. Earthworms have an instinct to burrow in the ground. Human babies have an instinct to start crying when they are hungry.

So how can you tell the difference between learned behaviors and instincts? Sometimes it is difficult. For example, humans have an instinct to speak a language. However, humans must learn to speak a particular language, such as English or Spanish. In this way, many behaviors are a mix of learning and instincts.

Other behaviors may be instinct alone. For example, very soon after a baby horse is born, it is able to stand up. Within a few hours, the baby horse can walk and run. The horse does not need to learn any part of this behavior. It is all instinctive.

Calves are born with an instinct to nurse by drinking milk from their mother.

Spiders have an instinct to spin webs.

Geese have an instinct to migrate south in the winter.

▶ Look at the behaviors below. Which are learned and which are instincts?

	Learned	Instinct
A parrot saying, "Hello"	○	○
A fish swimming	○	○
A racehorse running down a racetrack	○	○
A ground squirrel hibernating in the winter	○	○
A bee building a hive	○	○

Learning Your Lesson

You know a lot of things. You may know how to tie your shoes, how to read a clock, and how to add numbers. You were not born knowing these things. Instead, you learned them.

Active Reading As you read this page and the next, underline the examples of the skills you've learned.

Think of how learning keeps you from harm. For example, you know to look both ways before crossing the street. The ability to learn helps an animal survive. A **learned behavior** is something an animal learns from experience or by watching other animals.

▶ Pets are able to learn. What are some examples of tricks you could teach a pet?

- **To sit**
- **To stay**
- _____
- _____
- _____

202

© Houghton Mifflin Harcourt Publishing Company   (br) ©Getty Images/PhotoDisc

This chimpanzee is using a tool to get ants to eat. It probably learned to do this by watching other chimpanzees.

Playing baseball is a learned behavior. You have to learn the rules of the game. You also have to learn how to hit the ball with the bat.

Unlike instincts, learned behavior isn't always passed down from parent to child. For example, you can learn a language that your parent doesn't speak.

Many animals are able to learn things. Have you ever seen baby ducks following their mother? When the ducks first hatch, they learn to recognize their mother. After this, everywhere the mother goes, the babies follow. This helps keep the baby ducks safe.

Animals can also learn more complex behavior. Some chimpanzees learn how to make a tool for gathering termites to eat. They learn this by watching older chimpanzees make the tool from a branch. Without watching another chimpanzee do this, a young chimpanzee will not know how to make the tool.

Can you think of other examples of learned behavior? If you have a pet, think of things you have taught your pet to do. Also think about behaviors of working animals, such as horses and rescue dogs.

Sum It Up!

When you're done, use the answer key to check and revise your work.

Use the information in the summary to complete the graphic organizer.

Summarize

Heredity is the passing down of traits from parents to offspring. Inherited traits are controlled by genes. Traits can also be controlled by the environment. Traits can include physical characteristics. Hair color and feather color are traits passed down from parents to offspring. Traits can also include behaviors. Instincts are behaviors that an animal is born knowing how to do.

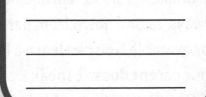

Main Idea: Heredity is the passing down of traits from parents to offspring.

Detail: Traits are controlled by genes and by the environment.

1 _____
_____
_____
_____

2 _____
_____
_____
_____

Answer Key: 1. Sample answer: Traits can include physical characteristics like hair color and feather color.
2. Sample answer: Traits can include behaviors such as instincts.

Name _____

Word Play

1 Use the words in the box to complete each sentence. Then use the circled letters to answer the question below.

gene	heredity*	instinct*
learned behavior*	offspring	traits

*Key Lesson Vocabulary

The passing of characteristics from parents to their young is known as

◯_ _ _ _ ◯_ _ .

An example of a _ _ _ _ _ _ _ ◯◯_ _ _ _ ◯
is a child learning to read.

A chemical instruction for a trait is known as a _ _◯_ .

Green eyes and red hair are examples of _ _◯_◯_ .

A bird chirping is an example of an ◯_ _ _ _ _ _ _ .

A living thing's children are also known as its ◯_ _ _ _ _ ◯_ .

Question:

Mice, ground squirrels, and other animals become inactive during the winter. What is the name of this instinctive behavior?

_ _ _ _ _ _ _ _ _ _ _

Apply Concepts

2 How can differences give some living things an advantage for survival and reproduction?

_____

_____

_____

_____

_____

3 List three examples of physical traits affected by the environment.

_____

_____

_____

_____

_____

_____

4 Draw and label a picture showing a learned behavior and a picture showing an instinctive behavior.

Learned Behavior	Instinct

Take It Home!

You perform many different learned behaviors daily. Keep a journal of some of the things you do in a week. Write down how you learned that behavior. For example, if you play tennis, record who taught you to play.

4.3.2 Observe, compare, and record the physical characteristics of living plants or animals from widely different environments, and describe how each is adapted to its environment.

Lesson **2**

Essential Question

How Are Living Things Adapted to Their Environment?

Engage Your Brain!

Find the answer to the following question in this lesson and record it here.

How do this fox's characteristics help it survive in its environment?

_____

_____

_____

_____

Active Reading

Lesson Vocabulary

List each term. As you learn about each one, make notes in the Interactive Glossary.

_____

_____

Signal Words: Details

This lesson gives details about the types of adaptations that help plants and animals survive in different environments. Signal words link main topics to added details. *For example, like,* and *for instance* are often used as signal words. Active readers look for signal words that link a topic to its details.

Life on the Blue Planet

Because most of Earth is covered in water, it is often called the Blue Planet. Life is found in water, on land, and everywhere in between!

Active Reading As you read this page, circle signal words that indicate details about the environment.

The **environment** is all of the living and nonliving things in nature. Look at the picture on this page. The environment shown here includes the animals, plants, water, soil, air, and everything else in the picture. Animals and plants depend on their environment to meet their needs. For example, the zebra in the picture gets its food, water, and shelter from its environment.

Earth has many different types of environments. For instance, some are very cold. Others are very hot. Some types of environments are deep in the ocean. Others are on dry land with very little rainfall. Because there are so many different types of environments on Earth, there are also many different types of living things. Each living thing is able to survive in its own environment.

All living things need food, water, air, and shelter. In dry places, living things must share the resources that are available.

Earth's different environments are home to many different kinds of living things. Notice how this mountain goat's environment is different from the zebra's environment.

Do the Math!

Percentages

The biggest environment on Earth is the ocean. That's because water covers about 70% of Earth's surface. The rest is land. Use this information to calculate how much of Earth's surface is land, and label the circle graph below.

Who Is out on a Limb?

Imagine you are in a forest. Which bird would you expect to see up in the trees: a blue jay or an ostrich?

Active Reading As you read this page, underline the definition of *adaptation*.

If you guessed a blue jay, you are right! Blue jays are small and have feet that can easily grip tree branches. Ostriches are large and have long legs and wide, strong feet. In other words, blue jays have adaptations that help them live in trees, while ostriches do not. An **adaptation** is a characteristic that helps a living thing survive.

Prairie dogs have long claws for digging burrows. Their brown color helps them blend into their grassland environment.

This ostrich lives in a grassland. Its long, strong legs allow it to run fast in wide open spaces. Its brown color helps it to blend in.

Living things that live in different environments have different adaptations. Living things in forests have adaptations for life in and around trees. Forest animals often have adaptations for gripping branches. Forest plants have adaptations that help them get light. For example, vines climb up trees.

Plants and animals that live in wide open spaces have different adaptations. Grasses are adapted to bend in strong winds. Grassland animals have adaptations for blending with the grass. Grassland animals may also run fast or have shovel-like paws for burrowing.

This blue jay's small, curved feet allow it to grip small branches. Its wings allow it to fly from branch to branch.

This sloth is adapted for life in trees. Its strong claws help it to hang from tree branches almost its entire life. Sloths can even sleep without letting go of the branch.

▶ Compare the prairie dog's grassland adaptations with the sloth's forest adaptations.

_____

_____

_____

_____

_____

_____

_____

_____

Who Can Take the Heat?

Deserts are places that get very little rain. Many deserts are very hot. How do plants and animals live in such dry, hot places?

Active Reading As you read the next two pages, circle the words used to describe desert and polar environments.

Desert plants and animals have adaptations that help them stay cool and conserve water. Many desert plants, like the cacti shown here, have wax coatings on their stems to help stop water loss. Many desert plants have very deep roots that can reach water that is deep underground. When it rains, desert plants make seeds quickly so the seeds have water.

Many reptiles, such as this horned lizard, live in the desert. The lizard's scales keep it from losing water.

Jack rabbits have large ears. This helps the rabbit release body heat and keeps the rabbit cool.

212

Animals often pant to stay cool. Many desert animals do not pant to avoid losing water. Most desert animals are active at night to avoid the heat of the day. They often have short, thin fur, or no fur at all.

Polar environments are very cold places. Plants and animals that live here are adapted to extremely cold winters and very short summers. Polar plants have short roots because the ground is frozen most of the year. Like desert plants, they make seeds quickly, during the short summer.

Polar animals have thick fur and a thick layer of fat to keep in body heat. Polar animals are often white, which helps them blend with their environment.

Arctic hares have white fur in the winter so they blend in with the snow. Their small ears and thick fur help keep them warm.

▶ Compare the jack rabbit's adaptations with the arctic hare's adaptations.

_____

_____

_____

_____

_____

Penguins have a thick layer of fat under their skin. They also have stiff, tightly-packed feathers. Both of these adaptations keep penguins warm in cold polar waters.

Who Can Go with the Flow?

Some are swimming upstream while others float with the breeze. What adaptations do living things need in different water environments?

Active Reading As you read the paragraph below, circle fish adaptations that help them live in a stream.

Imagine you lived in a constantly flowing stream of water. How could you stay in the same part of the stream without being carried away? Many fish living in streams have smooth bodies and strong tails. This helps them swim against the current. Water plants have flexible stems that allow them to bend with the flow. Many water insects are able to hold on tightly to water plants. Others burrow into soil at the bottom of the stream.

This fish has a smooth, streamlined body. Its body shape helps it swim quickly in fast moving water.

Elodea is very flexible, so flowing water is less likely to break it. If a piece of elodea is pulled off, though, the piece can sprout roots and start growing in a new part of the stream.

Plants growing in still water, such as ponds and lakes, have different adaptations. Some are tall with strong stems, so they can grow above the water. Others, like water lilies, float on the surface.

Animals that live in lakes and ponds are excellent swimmers. Many are adapted to living in deep water with little light. Cat fish have whiskers that sense chemicals in the water. This helps them find food in the dark. Some birds wade at the shore and hunt. Their long, thin legs look like the cattails, so fish do not see them until it's too late.

Cattails grow in relatively still, shallow water, such as the water of a pond. Their stems are strong and stiff. Cattails can grow over 3 m tall.

Pond turtles are strong swimmers. They are also able to hold their breath for long periods of time. Their dark color helps them stay hidden in dark, muddy water.

▶ Compare elodea's adaptations with the cattail's adaptations.

_____

_____

_____

_____

_____

When you're done, use the answer key to check and revise your work.

The outline below is a summary of the lesson. Complete the outline.

Summarize

I. Environment: All of the living and nonliving things in an area make up the environment. Parts of the environment include

A. _____

B. _____

C. _____

D. _____

E. _____

II. Adaptation: A characteristic that helps a living thing survive is called an adaptation. Kinds of adaptations include

A. Forest Adaptation: _____

B. Grassland Adaptation: _____

C. Desert Adaptation: _____

D. Polar Adaptation: _____

E. Underwater Adaptation: _____

Answer key: Sample answers: I.A. Animals; I.B. Plants; I.C. Water; I.D. Soil; I.E. Air; II.A. camouflaged fur; II.B. long claws for digging burrows; II.C. scaly skin to stop water loss; II.D. thick fur to stay warm; II.E. suction disc mouth to hold onto a rock in flowing water

Word Play

1 Use the words in the box to complete the puzzle.

Across

3. What is another name of a helpful characteristic an animal can have that helps it survive?

5. In what type of environment would a plant with spines, wax-coated leaves, and a large root system most likely be found?

Down

1. In what type of environment would birds with long legs for running most likely be found?

2. What do all the living and nonliving things in an area make up?

4. In what type of environment would an animal with a thick layer of fat and thick fur most likely be found?

Apply Concepts

2 Draw a circle around the plant that would most likely live in a forest environment. On the line below, list an adaptation the plant has that helps it live in a forest.

_____

3 Draw a circle around the animal that would most likely live in a desert environment. On the line below, list an adaptation the animal has that would help it live in a desert.

_____

4

What type of environment do you think this animal lives in? Explain your answer.

_____

_____

5 Snakes and lizards are rarely found living near polar regions. Why do you think this is the case?

_____

_____

_____

Take It Home!

Go on a walk through your neighborhood or a local park with your family. Look at different plants and animals, and point out different adaptations that the plants or animals have to help them survive.

Inquiry Flipchart page 22

Lesson **3**
INQUIRY

4.3.3 Design an investigation to explore
how organisms meet some of their needs
by responding to stimuli from their environment. **Nature of Science**

Name _____

Essential Question

How Do Organisms Respond to Their Environment?

Set a Purpose
Why is it important that animals be able to
respond to their environment?

_____

_____

_____

Write a statement summarizing some
needs that you think isopods have.

_____

_____

Think About the Procedure
What different things will you be doing to
see how the isopods will respond?

_____

_____

How do you predict the isopods will
respond to the changes in environment?

_____

_____

_____

Record Your Data
In the space below, make a data table for
your observations for each investigation.

Draw Conclusions

How did the isopods respond to the lamp?
How many responded the same way?

_____

_____

_____

_____

How did the isopods respond to the potato
and celery leaf?

_____

_____

_____

_____

Did all of the isopods respond the same
way to the potato and celery leaf?

_____

_____

_____

Analyze and Extend

1. How do you think isopods would
   respond to being touched?

   _____

   _____

   _____

2. How might the isopods' response
   to food help them survive in
   their environment?

   _____

   _____

   _____

3. How might the isopods' response
   to shade help them survive in
   their environment?

   _____

   _____

   _____

4. What other questions could you ask to
   investigate isopod behavior?

   _____

   _____

   _____

4.3.4 Describe a way that a given plant or animal might adapt to changes arising from human or non-human impact on the environment.

Lesson 4

Essential Question

How Do Living Things Adapt to Human Impact?

Engage Your Brain!

Find the answer to the following question in this lesson and record it here.

How has this animal adapted to survive in a human community?

_____

_____

_____

Active Reading

Lesson Vocabulary

List each term. As you learn about each one, make notes in the Interactive Glossary.

_____

_____

Typographical Clues

This lesson has several words that are highlighted in yellow or italicized. Highlighting or italicizing are types of typographical clues. Active readers look for typographical clues that indicate a word is a vocabulary word or an important term.

Making an Impact

Can you think of a place on Earth where humans haven't been? Chances are your list will be very short!

Active Reading   As you read the next page, underline the definition of *pollution*.

In one way or another, human activity has affected almost every environment on Earth. As the human population grows, it takes up more and more land. People use land for homes and businesses and for growing food. The more land we use, the less space is available for wildlife.

Acid rain has killed the trees on this mountain.

Many human activities result in waste products. These wastes can be harmful to the living things in the environment. **Pollution** is any harmful substance in the environment.

Examples of pollution include trash, chemicals, smoke, heat, noise, and even light. Pollution in the air can make the air unsafe to breathe. For example, automobile exhaust in large cities makes the air harmful to people. Pollution on land and in water can kill plants and animals, and make water unsafe to drink. Other types of pollution, such as noise and light, disrupt the activities of animals in the area. Noise and light make it hard for animals to find mates or to find their way home.

What's Changed?

How do you think the land in the photo of the city was different before humans built on it?

_____

_____

_____

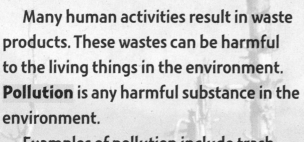

When fossil fuels are burned for energy, chemicals in the smoke enter the air. These chemicals combine with water in the air to form acid. The result is acid rain that is strong enough to wear away statues, like the lion shown here.

Getting Along with the Neighbors

When people move in, not everyone moves out. Many living things adapt to life among humans.

Active Reading As you read the next page, underline the sentence describing how songbirds can adapt to city life.

These storks keep their eggs out of reach of predators by building their nest on the top of a chimney.

People pave surfaces, but plants soon start growing in any cracks. Over time, roots will break pavement in the same way that they weather rocks.

There are many ways that living things have adapted to human impact. Some songbirds living in loud cities change their songs so their mates can still hear them. Many animals learn to use human-made materials to build nests, or find shelter in buildings. Many animals, like raccoons, eat the food that people throw out. Animals have even learned to break into houses and cars to steal food!

Insects are well adapted to city life. They are found in lawns and trees, in the cupboards of houses, and even on pets. People use chemicals to kill insects, but often some survive. They have young that, like their parents, might not be affected by the chemicals. The same thing happens with plants that people consider pests. Over time, weed-killing chemicals become less effective as plants adapt to them.

Sunken ships provide a home for many kinds of ocean life.

Make Yourself at Home

Think of a plant or animal you have seen around your town. How has this living thing adapted to humans?

_____

_____

_____

_____

_____

Going, Going, Gone

Some plants and animals are becoming more and more rare. What happens if there are none left?

As you read these two pages, underline what happens when living things cannot adapt to a changed environment.

Some plants and animals are not able to adapt to changes in the environment. These living things are in danger of dying out. **Extinction** happens when there are none left of a certain type of animal or plant.

Since life first appeared on Earth, millions of living things have become extinct as a result of natural changes to the environment. Now, many have become extinct or are in danger of becoming extinct as a result of human activities.

Polar bears live in the Arctic, a frozen environment to the north. As temperatures on Earth keep rising, the polar bear's environment is changing. What might happen to the polar bears?

Do the Math!
Interpret Graphs

The destruction of wetlands along the Gulf Coast caused whooping cranes to almost die out. In 1955 there were only 21 left! People have worked to save them by building safe places for cranes to live. The government has also passed laws to protect them. The graph shows how the whooping crane has recovered.

Whooping Crane Population

1. About how long did it take the number of cranes to increase from 100 to 200? _____
2. What could happen if people stop protecting the whopping crane?

_____

The Tasmanian wolf lived in Australia. Ranchers thought the wolves were eating sheep. All of the Tasmanian wolves were hunted and are presumed extinct.

This purple fringed orchid is native to the United States. However, agriculture and non-native plants use the space needed by native plants. Because of this, the orchid is at risk of becoming extinct.

Giving Nature a Helping Hand

Humans can have a positive impact on the environment. Many human activities help living things survive.

Active Reading As you read the next page, underline the definition of *conservation*.

Community gardens like this one provide food for people to eat, places for animals to live, and help clean the air.

Living things depend on other living things for survival. People depend on plants and animals for food and many of the things we use every day. We also appreciate wildlife and nature for its own beauty. So people work to protect plants and animals from dying out. **Conservation** is the protection and wise use of natural resources, including plants and animals.

One of the main ways people conserve wildlife and plant life is by providing places that offer protection. Parks are set aside so living things can survive without being disturbed by human activities. In the United States, there are hundreds of national parks, thousands of state parks, and thousands of local parks that provide safe places for animals and plants to live.

Cleaning up trash keeps pollution from harming wildlife.

But not all living things are in parks. As you have learned, plants and animals live along with people in cities and towns. People use native plants for landscaping to provide food and shelter for native wildlife, including butterflies and birds. Some cities set aside paths for animals to move from one natural area to another without crossing highways. Engineers design bridges with places for bats to nest. There are many ways people work to protect living things from human impact.

DO NOT DISTURB SEA TURTLE NEST

VIOLATORS SUBJECT TO FINES AND IMPRISONMENT

U.S. ENDANGERED SPECIES ACT OF 1973

Signs like this one protect sea turtle nests from accidentally being stepped on.

Making a Difference

What are some ways that you can have a positive impact on the environment?

_____

_____

_____

_____

229

Sum It Up!

When you're done, use the answer key to check and revise your work.

Read the summary statements below. Each one is incorrect.
Change the part of the summary in blue to make it correct.

1 As cities grow, they tend to take up less land.

_____
_____

2 Pollution that can harm wildlife includes air, water, soil, rocks, and plants.

_____
_____

3 Over time, weed-killing chemicals become more effective as plants adapt to them.

_____
_____

4 Many types of animals living in human communities eat only food found in forests and other natural areas.

_____
_____

5 If living things are unable to adapt to changes in the environment, they may become pets.

_____
_____

6 One way to help urban wildlife is to plant fancy flowers.

_____
_____

Answer Key: 1. spread out over more land; 2. dangerous trash, chemicals, noise, heat, and light 3. less effective; 4. food that people throw out; 5. extinct 6. native plants

Name _____

Word Play

1 Draw lines to match the words in the column on the left to the correct description on the right.

1. conservation

2. extinction

3. wildlife reserve

4. acid rain

5. pollution

6. urban wildlife

A. land set aside to provide a safe place for living things to survive

B. anything harmful in the environment

C. plants and animals that have adapted to living in human communities

D. to completely die out

E. rain polluted with chemicals that have combined with water in the air

F. the preservation and wise use of resources

Apply Concepts

2 What are some of the ways humans have changed the environment in the picture below?

_____

_____

3 Below each picture, describe how the living thing has adapted to changes made in the environment by humans.

_____ _____ _____ _____

_____ _____ _____ _____

_____ _____ _____ _____

4 What type of animals do you think would have the most difficulty adapting to life in a human community?

_____

_____

_____

5 People change the land to build shopping centers, schools, or homes. How do the animals that once lived on that land survive?

_____

_____

Take It Home!

Research different animals that live in human communities. Choose one animal, and draw a picture showing how it has adapted to changes made in the environment by humans.

4.3.3 Design an investigation to explore how organisms meet some of their needs by responding to stimuli from their environment. **4.3.4** Describe a way that a given plant or animal might adapt to changes arising from human or non-human impact on the environment.

People in Science

Meet the Tree-Planting Scientists

Wangari Maathai

Wangari Maathai was born in Kenya. Maathai started an organization that conserves Kenya's forests by planting trees. She recruited Kenyan women to plant native trees throughout the country. In 1977, this organization became known as the Green Belt Movement. The Green Belt Movement has planted more than 40 million trees. Maathai's work inspires other African countries to start community tree plantings.

Seeds from nearby forests are used to grow native trees.

Willie Smits

Willie Smits works to save orangutans in Indonesia. By clearing the forests, people are destroying the orangutan's habitat. The orangutan is endangered. Smits's plan helps both orangutans and people. Smits is growing a rain forest. The new forest gives people food and rainwater for drinking, so they protect it. The sugar palm is one of the trees planted. In 2007, Smits started using sugar palms to make sugar and a biofuel called ethanol. The sugar palms provide income for the community.

Sugar palms are fire-resistant. This protects the forest from fires.

Smits has rescued almost 1,000 orangutan babies. However, his goal is to save them in the wild.

233

Scientist saves the Day!

Read the story about the Florida scrub jay. Draw the missing pictures to complete the story.

The Problem: Florida scrub jays are endangered. They are found only in parts of Florida with shrubs and other short plants.

Fires kill tall trees that grow in the scrub jay's habitat. But people put out the fires, so the trees survive.

Trees are now growing, so there are fewer shrubs. The scrub jays can't live there.

The Solution: Scientists and firefighters start fires that can be kept under control. These fires kill the tall trees.

Shrubs grow and the scrub jays return.

Multiple Choice

4.3.1

1 Monarch butterflies migrate to warm places every winter. What causes this?

(A) trait

(B) instinct

(C) characteristic

(D) learned behavior

4.3.1

2 The pictures below show animal behaviors. Which one is a learned behavior?

(A)

(B)

(C)

(D)

4.3.1

3 The hummingbird uses its long beak to get nectar from flowers. What term BEST identifies the hummingbird's long beak?

(A) a gene

(B) a trait

(C) a learned behavior

(D) an inherited characteristic

4.3.1

4 Suppose Ada could play the clarinet by instinct. Which sentence describes what Ada would do?

(A) Ada would have to practice a lot.

(B) Ada would need a clarinet teacher.

(C) Ada would know how to play the drums.

(D) Ada would play well the first time she tried.

4.3.1

5 Parents pass on traits to their children. What are traits?

(A) genes

(B) instincts

(C) learned behavior

(D) physical characteristics

4.3.1

6 Which adaptation will MOST LIKELY be found in animals that live in polar environments?

(A) white fur

(B) large ears

(C) bushy tail

(D) sharp claws

4.3.2

7 Which adaptation will MOST LIKELY be found in animals that live in trees?

Ⓐ white fur

Ⓑ moist skin

Ⓒ sharp teeth

Ⓓ grasping feet

4.3.2

8 Which adaptation will MOST LIKELY be found in a desert plant?

Ⓐ thin leaves that provide shade

Ⓑ leaves that produce a lot of water

Ⓒ branches that hang down and shed water

Ⓓ deep roots that reach water below ground

4.3.2

9 Which adaptation does a whale have that helps it live under water?

Ⓐ hair

Ⓑ flippers

Ⓒ sharp teeth

Ⓓ large body

4.3.2

10 Which adaptation would BEST help an animal hunt other animals for food?

Ⓐ large feet

Ⓑ bushy tail

Ⓒ colorful fur

Ⓓ keen eyesight

Nature of Science, 4.3.3

11 Crickets chirp by rubbing their legs together. The table below has information about chirping in crickets.

Temperature (°C)	Number of chirps in 15 sec
17	26
19	29
20	31
24	37
32	50

What can you conclude about the effect of temperature on chirping in crickets?

Ⓐ The number of chirps decreases as temperature goes up.

Ⓑ The number of chirps does not change with temperature.

Ⓒ The number of chirps goes up as the temperature goes up.

Ⓓ The number of chirps goes up and down as temperature goes up.

4.3.3

12 The green anole is a lizard. Outside, the anole may be green on a lawn, but it will have a brown color on dirt. This change in color protects the anole from predators. This change in color also shows something about the anole's physical features. What does a change in the anole's color show?

Ⓐ Physical features are inherited.

Ⓑ The environment can affect physical features.

Ⓒ Anoles depend on changes in color for reproduction.

Ⓓ Anoles are more likely to encounter predators indoors.

Nature of Science, 4.3.3

13 The picture below shows two plants. Plant 1 was grown in the dark. Plant 2 was grown in the light.

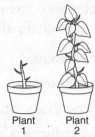

Plant 1   Plant 2

What can you conclude about the growth of these plants?

Ⓐ The environment can affect physical features.

Ⓑ The environment determines all physical features.

Ⓒ The environment plays no role in the growth of plants.

Ⓓ The environment determines which structures a plant will have.

4.3.3

14 The table below has information about egg laying in monarch butterflies.

Number of Monarch Eggs

Day	Plant A	Plant B
1	59	0
2	7	1
3	22	0
4	11	2

What can you conclude about egg laying in monarch butterflies?

Ⓐ Monarch butterflies lay more eggs as time goes on.

Ⓑ Monarch butterflies prefer Plant A for laying their eggs.

Ⓒ Monarch butterflies prefer Plant B for laying their eggs.

Ⓓ Monarch butterflies have no preference about which plant they lay their eggs on.

Nature of Science, 4.3.3

15 Sam went out at night to search for earthworms. He shined his flashlight on the ground and saw dozens of earthworms. What is the BEST explanation for what Sam saw?

Ⓐ Earthworms are attracted to flashlights.

Ⓑ Earthworms come out of the ground to escape being eaten.

Ⓒ Earthworms stay in moist places to keep from drying out.

Ⓓ Earthworms come out at night because they prefer darkness.

4.3.4

16 Chanda's garden is overrun with Japanese beetles. The beetles are eating all her plants. She tries to get rid of the beetles by spraying them, but most of them survive. What is the BEST explanation for Chanda's problem?

Ⓐ Japanese beetles are very hungry.

Ⓑ Japanese beetles like the plants in Chanda's garden best.

Ⓒ People have never tried spraying Japanese beetles to get rid of them.

Ⓓ People have sprayed Japanese beetles before, and now most are not affected by the spray.

4.3.4

17 The animal in the picture lives in bamboo forests and eats mostly bamboo.

What will MOST LIKELY happen to it if the bamboo forests are all cut down?

Ⓐ It will die out.

Ⓑ It will have more babies.

Ⓒ It will move to a different area.

Ⓓ It will hunt other animals for food.

4.3.4

18 The ice at the North Pole gives polar bears a place to live. The ice is slowly melting. What will MOST LIKELY happen to polar bears as a result?

Ⓐ Polar bears will not be affected by the melting of the ice.

Ⓑ Polar bears will move to the South Pole where there is more ice.

Ⓒ Polar bears may die out because there will not be enough ice to support them.

Ⓓ Polar bears will increase in numbers because their food will become easier to catch.

4.3.4

19 Humans cause changes in the environment. Sometimes, animals can adapt to these changes. Which of these statements is the BEST example of animals adapting to these changes?

Ⓐ Ducks swim in streams.

Ⓑ Falcons nest on skyscrapers.

Ⓒ Squirrels bury nuts for winter.

Ⓓ Dogs catch flying discs in a park.

4.3.4

20 Humans cause changes in the environment. Sometimes, plants can adapt to these changes. Which of these statements is the BEST example of plants adapting to human activity?

Ⓐ Trees grow in a forest.

Ⓑ Corn grows in an open field.

Ⓒ Cacti grown in the desert.

Ⓓ Weeds grow when treated with weed killer.

Constructed Response

4.3.1

21 Samantha has brown hair, but her younger brother, Nicholas, has black hair. Why is it important to know they are brother and sister when comparing hair color?

_____

_____

Give a reason why they have different color hair even though they have the same parents.

_____

_____

4.3.2

22 Animals that live in desert areas have different adaptations from animals that live in polar areas. List two ways a rabbit that lives in the desert might differ from a rabbit that lives in a polar environment.

(1) _____

_____

_____

(2) _____

_____

_____

4.3.4

23 Some kinds of mosquitoes are resistant to pesticides. Spraying pesticides on these mosquitoes does not kill them. What is likely to happen to the mosquito population over time if the same pesticide is used?

_____

_____

_____

Describe the cycle this type of adaptation could cause?

_____

_____

_____

Extended Response

4.3.4

24 Hannah is studying the number of tigers that live in the wild. She found information on two kinds of tigers. One lives in northern Asia. The other lives in southern Asia. Her data are listed below. Use the data to complete the table.

In 1986, there were 300 tigers in northern Asia and 80 in southern Asia.

In 1996, there were 230 tigers in northern Asia and 30 in southern Asia.

In 1998, there were 406 tigers in northern Asia and 30 in southern Asia.

In 2004, there were 450 tigers in northern Asia and 0 tigers in southern Asia.

Number of Tigers		
Year		

According to the table, which tiger population has remained about the same in number?

_____

_____

According to the table, which tiger has died out?

_____

_____

Give ONE reason why an animal living in the wild could die out.

_____

_____

Nature of Science, 4.3.3

25 James investigated how cockroaches respond to light. He put cockroaches into a cage. One side of the cage was dark, and the other side had a light. James recorded the number of cockroaches in each side of the cage for four different trials. His results are shown in the table below.

Cockroach Choices—Light or Dark

Trial	Cockroaches in Light	Cockroaches in Dark
1	10	30
2	20	20
3	0	40
4	5	35

How many cockroaches did James test altogether?

_____

_____

During which trials were there more cockroaches in the dark?

_____

_____

According to the data, do cockroaches like dark places or lighted places better?

_____

_____

What is one possible explanation for the preference shown by cockroaches for light or dark?

_____

_____

_____

Forces and Transportation

STANDARD 4
Science, Engineering and Technology

PROCESS STANDARDS
Design Process

Indianapolis Motor Speedway

I Wonder Why

Why do the Indianapolis 500 race cars have pointy noses and tails on the back? *Turn the page to find out.*

Here's Why The pointy nose on race cars reduces wind resistance and the tail helps to keep the wheels on the ground.

Track Your Progress

Essential Questions and Indiana Standards

STANDARD 4
Science, Engineering and Technology

PROCESS STANDARDS
Design Process

Design a moving system and measure its motion.

As citizens of the constructed world, students will participate in the design process. Students will learn to use materials and tools safely and employ the basic principles of the engineering design process in order to find solutions to problems.

4.4.1 Investigate transportation systems and devices that operate on or in land, water, air and space and recognize the forces (lift, drag, friction, thrust and gravity) that affect their motion.
4.4.2 Make appropriate measurements to compare the speeds of objects in terms of distance traveled in a given amount of time or time required to travel a given distance.

Essential Question
What Is Motion?

Engage Your Brain!

As you read the lesson, figure out the answer to the following question. Write the answer here.

Is it moving if it's not going anywhere? How can you describe the motion of this hovering hummingbird?

_____

_____

_____

_____

_____

_____

Active Reading

Lesson Vocabulary
List the terms. As you learn about each one, make notes in the Interactive Glossary.

_____   _____

_____   _____

_____   _____

Main Idea and Details
Detail sentences give information about a main idea. The details may be examples, features, characteristics, or facts. Active readers stay focused on the topic when they ask, What fact or other information does this detail add to the main idea?

243

Twisting and Turning

What tells you the person below in the picture is moving? Is it possible for a person to move in more than one direction at a time? You can find out!

Curve

The boy's body moves in a curved path around the bar.

The blurry lines show you the directions in which the girl is moving.

Straight Line

As the girl flips down the balance beam, she moves in a straight line.

How would you describe where your left hand is right now? Is it on top of your book or is it touching your chin? Can you think of a way to describe where your left hand is without referring to something else near it? No. **Position** is the location of an object in relation to a nearby object or place. The second object or place is called the *reference point*.

Now put your left hand in a different place. This change in position is **motion**. To describe your hand's motion, you'd tell in what direction it moved from its earlier position, as well as how fast it moved. The girl in the picture is in motion. Parts of her body are moving up and down while other parts move in a circle. And, overall, her body moves forward in a straight line.

Moving and Going Nowhere?

Draw a picture of something that only moves back and forth.

Where Is It?

How can you tell the penguin is moving?

Active Reading As you read the next page, underline the words that describe specific reference points.

1. The penguin has just jumped from the top of the ice.

2. The penguin is between the top of the ice and the water.

3. The penguin is entering the water.

You know something is moving if its position changes against a background. The background is called the *frame of reference*.

The picture of the penguin shows three images taken as the penguin jumped off the ice. Notice that each image of the penguin has the same frame of reference. You can choose any part of that background as a reference point. The words *top of the ice* describe the reference point for Image 1. Both *top of the ice* and *the water* describe reference points for Image 2. Only *the water* describes a reference point for Image 3.

What if the images of the penguin had been in the wrong order? Could you put them in the correct order? Sure! You know that things don't fall up, so you could use the water as the reference point for each image. The image of the penguin highest above the water must be first. The image of the penguin closest to the water is last.

Look at the pictures of the horse race. In the pictures, what can you use for reference points? How can you use the reference points to put the pictures in order?

▶ Put these pictures in order by writing numbers in the circles. Then explain how you decided on the order.

_____

_____

_____

_____

5 meters

0	5	10	15	20	25	30	35	40	45

Ready! Set! Go!

00:00 → **00:10**

The turtle, cat, and rabbit start running at the same time. How far does each of them go in 10 seconds?

Fast and Slow?

Could a turtle beat a rabbit in a race?
It depends on each animal's speed.

Active Reading As you read this page, underline the definitions of *speed* and *velocity*.

One way to describe motion is to find speed, or how fast or slow something is moving. **Speed** tells you how the position of an object changes during a certain amount of time. You can measure time in hours (hr), minutes (min), or seconds (sec).

To find an object's speed, you divide how far it goes by the time it takes to get there. So if you walk 30 meters (m) in 15 seconds (sec), your speed is 2 m/sec.

{ 30 m ÷ 15 sec = 2 m/sec }

How is velocity different from speed? **Velocity** is the speed of an object in a particular direction. Suppose you walk toward the east. If your speed is 2 m/sec, then your velocity is 2 m/sec, east.

In a race on a straight track, all the runners move in the same direction. Their velocities differ only because their speeds differ. Could a turtle win a race against a rabbit? Sure! The rabbit could run very fast in the wrong direction!

| 50 | 55 | 60 | 65 | 70 | 75 | 80 | 85 | 90 | 95 | 100 |

80 meters

100 meters

Do the Math!
Calculate Speed

1. What is the speed of the rabbit during the race?

_____

2. What is the speed of the turtle during the race?

_____

3. A chicken joins the race and runs at 4 m/sec. On the distance line, draw the chicken where it would be after 10 seconds.

_____

_____

_____

_____

Changing It Up

The gas pedal on a car is called an accelerator. Did you know that the brakes and steering wheel are also accelerators?

Active Reading As you read these pages, circle three phrases that tell how an object can accelerate.

Y ou may hear people say that a car is accelerating when it speeds up. That's only partly correct. **Acceleration** is any change in velocity. Remember that velocity tells both the speed and the direction of motion. So matter accelerates if it speeds up, slows down, or changes direction.

Acceleration of any kind is caused by forces. A **force** is any kind of push or pull affecting an object. If a force pushing against an object in one direction is greater than a force pushing in the opposite direction, the object will accelerate.

Turn and Speed Up

In this section, the fly accelerates because it changes both its direction and its speed.

Look at the path of the fly. The fly accelerates each time it changes either its speed or its direction. Sometimes it changes both its speed and its direction at the same time!

Slow Down

Here, the fly is traveling in a straight line while slowing down. This is also acceleration.

Speed Up

In this section of its path, the fly travels in a straight line. It accelerates because it is speeding up.

Stop and Start

The fly lands on the wall and stops moving. Its body doesn't accelerate. When it starts moving again, it speeds up. So, it accelerates.

Change Direction

The fly's speed stays the same as it changes direction. Because its velocity changes, it accelerates.

▶ Fill in the missing parts of the table.

Item	Speed	What happens?	Acceleration?
Mouse	1 m/sec	suddenly chased by a cat	
Runner	8 m/sec	runs at the same speed around a circular track	
Train	80 km/hr	moves along a straight track	
Jet plane	300 km/hr		Yes, slows down.

Pushes and Pulls

Gravity

Gravity pulls down with a force that keeps the truck on the road.

Sand

Pushing, pulling, sliding, rolling, falling... What do all these actions have in common?

Active Reading As you read these two pages, draw circles around the names of two types of forces.

What have you pushed or pulled today? Maybe you pushed open a door or pulled on your shoes. A push or a pull is a force. Suppose you want to change the way something is moving. A force can change an object's speed or direction.

Many forces act on you. *Gravity* is a force that pulls objects down to Earth. Gravity keeps you on the ground or on a chair.

Friction is a force that acts directly against the direction of motion. Friction can slow things down or make them stop.

252

▶ Why do you think workers spread sand on icy, snow-covered roads?

_____

Force

The force of the truck tires pulling on the road moves the truck forward.

Friction

The snow exerts a force of friction that pushes backward against the truck and slows it down.

▶ Look at the girl on the sled. Draw arrows and label *gravity*, *force*, and *friction*.

Forces in Your Car

You may not have ridden in a dump truck spreading sand. But you've ridden in a car as it drove down a road. The forces in action are much the same.

spoiler

Down Force

When cars are going fast, it's important for the tires to grip the road. To help with this, some fast cars have spoilers on the back. As air rushes over a spoiler, the force of the air pushes the car downward. This helps the back tires stay firmly on the ground.

Friction

Without friction, the car wouldn't move.

The car's engine applies a force to the wheels, which makes them turn. In the United States, the strength of this force is measured in a unit called horsepower.

The force of gravity acts on the car, too. The more a car weighs, the more horsepower the engine has to apply to get it moving.

The force of friction acts where the tires touch the road. Without friction, there can be no acceleration. Picture a car on a sheet of ice. There's no friction between the tires and the ice. The tires spin, but the car doesn't go anywhere.

Once the car is moving, another force comes into play. The car is moving through air. As the car pushes against the air, the air pushes back against the car, slowing it down. Most people call this force "air resistance." In science, it's called **drag**.

▶ Add an arrow representing drag to the illustration.

Thrust

Thrust is created when the engine turns the wheels.

Forces at Sea

The first thing you notice about a boat is that it floats. Why do some things float and others sink? It's all a matter of forces.

Active Reading As you read these two pages, find and underline the definition of *displace*.

Picture this: You fill a glass to the rim with tea. Then you put in a couple of ice cubes. What happens? Some of the tea slops over the sides of the glass.

If you think about it, it makes sense. The ice cubes take up room in the glass. But if the glass is already full of tea, some of the tea has to leave to make room for the ice.

Even if the glass isn't full, the ice still takes up space. Adding ice means moving some of the tea out of the way. When the ice goes in, the level of the tea rises.

This happens whenever you put a solid into a liquid. The solid displaces some of the liquid. **Displace** means to move away.

Over 2,200 years ago, a man named Archimedes figured out why objects float. The force of gravity pulls the object down. Water must exert an upward force on the object. Archimedes figured out that the upward force is equal to the weight of the water that the object displaces.

The ice cubes displaced some of the tea. That tea had nowhere to go but over the side.

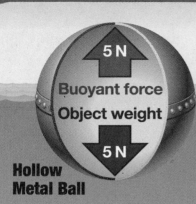

Hollow Metal Ball

5 N — Buoyant force / Object weight — 5 N

Floats

The empty ball weighs 5 Newtons. It would displace 10 N of water if it sank. So the ball floats.

10 N / 10 N

Neutral

If 5 N of steel balls are added, the ball weighs 10 N and displaces 10N of water. The ball hovers in the water, neither floating nor sinking.

Sinks

The ball full of steel weighs more than the water it's displacing. That's why it sinks.

10 N / 15 N

The upward force of water is called the **buoyant force**. If the buoyant force acting on an object is greater than the force of gravity acting on the object, the object floats. If the buoyant force is less than the force of gravity, the object sinks.

But how can a steel ship float? A solid block of steel would sink. But a ship has lots of open spaces inside. These spaces are filled with air. The steel and the air together weigh less than the water the ship displaces. That's why the ship floats.

Water Power

What happens if you force a beach ball under water? Why do you think this is?

_____

_____

_____

Why Things Fly

How can something that's made out of steel fly?
Again, it's all a matter of forces.

Air Flow

Plane wing moving forward

Pressure exerted by faster-moving air

Pressure exerted by slower-moving air

A ship floats when the force pushing it up is greater than the force pulling it down. The ship is pushed up by the buoyant force. It is pulled down by gravity. The same is true for airplanes. Except in this case, the upward force is called lift.

Lift is caused by air pushing against the plane's wings. If the lift force is greater than the plane's weight, the plane will rise. It takes to the air. But say the pilot does something to reduce lift. Now the weight is greater than the lift. The plane drops.

The diagram above shows a cross-section of an airplane wing. As the wing moves through the air, some air goes over it and some goes under it. Because of the shape of the wing, the air going over the wing moves faster than the air underneath. The faster the air moves, the less pressure it exerts. That means the air moving over the top of

Air Pressure

Up and Away

Rockets have no wings, so there is no lift. But they are affected by thrust, drag, and gravity. Draw these forces on the photo.

_____

_____

_____

_____

_____

_____

the wing exerts less pressure, and the air below the wing exerts more pressure. The difference between the two forces pushes the plane upward, producing lift.

This doesn't explain all flight. Some wings aren't shaped like this. And even planes with these wings can fly upside down. But this explains how most airplanes fly under most conditions.

There are two other forces that act on airplanes in flight. Just like the car and the dump truck, the plane's engine produces thrust. And if the plane is moving, air resistance produces drag.

Why Things Stay in Orbit

Thrust from the rockets gets a satellite into space.
Once the satellite is in orbit, it stays there.
What kind of forces make this possible?

Active Reading As you read these two pages, draw two lines under each main idea.

This satellite is in orbit high above Earth. It stays in orbit because its speed keeps it moving forward.

Imagine a cannon firing a cannon ball. The cannon exerts a force on the cannon ball. The ball travels a certain distance from the cannon before it hits the ground.

Then you add more powder to the cannon. The cannon exerts more force on the next cannon ball. This cannon ball travels farther before it hits the ground.

Now you add a lot more powder. The cannon exerts a lot of force on this cannon ball. The ball travels much farther. In fact, it goes all the way around the world and passes the cannon again. The cannon ball is in orbit. *Orbit* is the path an object travels around another object in space. Speed is the key to staying in orbit.

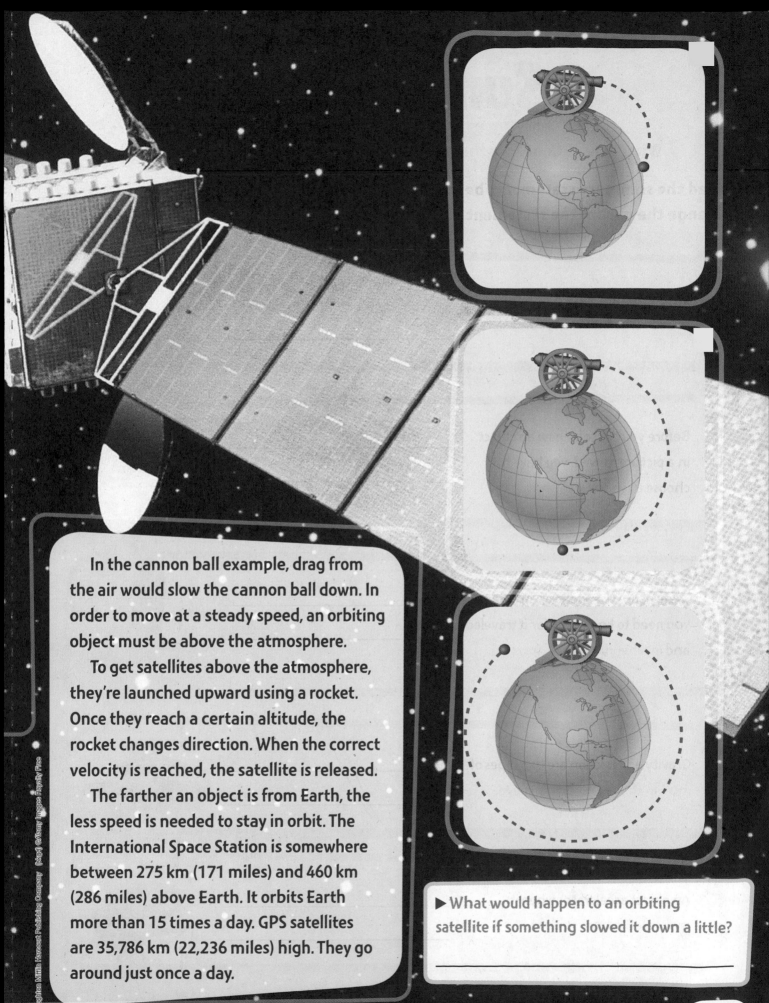

In the cannon ball example, drag from the air would slow the cannon ball down. In order to move at a steady speed, an orbiting object must be above the atmosphere.

To get satellites above the atmosphere, they're launched upward using a rocket. Once they reach a certain altitude, the rocket changes direction. When the correct velocity is reached, the satellite is released.

The farther an object is from Earth, the less speed is needed to stay in orbit. The International Space Station is somewhere between 275 km (171 miles) and 460 km (286 miles) above Earth. It orbits Earth more than 15 times a day. GPS satellites are 35,786 km (22,236 miles) high. They go around just once a day.

▶ What would happen to an orbiting satellite if something slowed it down a little?

_____

Sum It Up!

When you're done, use the answer key to check and revise your work.

Read the summary statements below. Each statement is incorrect. Change the part of the statement in blue to make it correct.

1 You know that something is in motion when it speeds up.
_____
_____

2 Before you describe how an object in a picture moved, you have to choose a type of motion.
_____
_____

3 To measure the speed of an object, you need to know how far it traveled and in what direction it traveled.
_____
_____

4 Gravity and friction are two types of motion that an object can have.
_____
_____

5 An object accelerates when it moves left or moves right.
_____
_____

Answer Key: 1. changes its position; 2. reference point; 3. how long it took; 4. forces that act on objects; 5. speeds up, slows down, or changes direction

Word Play

1 Important words from this lesson are scrambled in the following box. Unscramble the words. Place each word in a set of squares.

lcaoeciranet	despe	eerrfcnee	oitmon
hups	crefo	vatgiyr	ovltyiec

		c		

	r				

			o	

		c							

	s	

			r			

			d	

		o			

Rearrange the letters in the colored boxes to form a word that describes the location of an object.

Put a star next to two words that describe how fast something moves.

Apply Concepts

2 Describe the motion and path of the diver. Use the words *position*, *speed*, *velocity*, and *acceleration* in your description.

_____

_____

_____

_____

_____

_____

_____

_____

_____

_____

_____

3 You are riding in a bus. Your friend is standing on the street corner as the bus goes by. How would you describe the way your friend seems to move? How would your friend describe your motion? Why do the descriptions differ?

_____

_____

_____

_____

_____

4

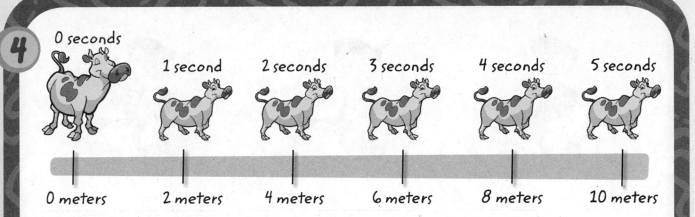

0 seconds   1 second   2 seconds   3 seconds   4 seconds   5 seconds

0 meters   2 meters   4 meters   6 meters   8 meters   10 meters

The diagram represents the motion of a cow walking in a straight line across a field. Use it to answer these questions.

a. Is the cow accelerating? Why or why not?

_____

_____

_____

_____

_____

_____

b. Calculate the speed of the cow.

_____

_____

_____

_____

c. How long will it take the cow to travel 24 meters? Describe how you found the correct answer.

_____

_____

_____

_____

_____

d. How far will the cow travel in 35 seconds? Describe how you found the correct answer.

_____

_____

_____

_____

_____

5 Describe three different forces that act on you as you walk. Draw an arrow on each picture to show the direction of a force. Make sure to include gravity and friction.

_____ _____ _____

_____ _____ _____

_____ _____ _____

_____ _____ _____

6 In each box, draw a picture that shows an object moving in the way described by the label at the top of the box. Describe the forces acting on the object.

Floating at Sea	Orbiting Earth

Take It Home!

Choose three places in your community. With a family member, visit each place and look for things that move. In a chart, record what you observe. Can you identify the forces causing the motion?

266

4.4.2 Make appropriate measurements to compare the speeds of objects in terms of distance traveled in a given amount of time or time required to travel a given distance. **4.4.3** Investigate how changes in speed or direction are caused by forces; the greater the force exerted on an object, the greater the change. **Nature of Science**

Name _____

Essential Question

What Is Speed?

Set a Purpose

What do you think you will learn from this experiment?

_____

_____

_____

State Your Hypothesis

Write your hypothesis, or testable statement.

_____

_____

_____

Think About the Procedure

How can you figure out the speed at which the ball is moving?

_____

_____

_____

As you pull the ball back farther each time, what happens to the force with which the ball is launched?

_____

_____

Record Your Data

In the space below, draw a table in which to record your observations.

Draw Conclusions

What conclusion can you draw from this investigation?

_____

_____

_____

Analyze and Extend

1. How can the same object move at different speeds?

_____

_____

_____

_____

2. What other factors might have affected the speed at which the ball moved?

_____

_____

_____

3. Are there limits to how much force you could apply to the ball in this inquiry? If so, what are they?

_____

_____

_____

_____

_____

4. What would you expect to happen if you were to use a larger rubber band?

_____

_____

_____

_____

_____

5. Think of other questions you would like to ask about speed and motion.

_____

_____

_____

_____

_____

4.4.3 Investigate how changes in speed or direction are caused by forces; the greater the force exerted on an object, the greater the change. **Nature of Science**

Name _____

Essential Question

Which Forces Affect Motion?

Set a Purpose

What do you think you will learn from this experiment?

_____

_____

_____

_____

_____

Think About the Procedure

What property of the car will you be changing when you attach the fishing weight?

_____

_____

What force will you be changing as you add materials to the surface of the board?

_____

_____

What does the reading on the meter stick represent?

_____

_____

Record Your Data

In the space below, draw a table in which to record your observations.

Draw Conclusions

What conclusion can you draw from this investigation?

_____

_____

_____

_____

Analyze and Extend

1. Imagine you have built a soapbox racer—an unpowered go-cart that races downhill. Will it go faster down a paved hill or a grassy hill with the same slope? Why?

_____

_____

_____

_____

2. Based on this experiment, what could you do to improve your soapbox racer's performance?

_____

_____

_____

_____

3. What might affect the motion of a full-sized soapbox racer on a 1 km downhill course that did not affect your model?

_____

_____

_____

_____

_____

_____

_____

4. Think of other questions you would like to ask about forces and motion.

_____

_____

_____

_____

_____

_____

_____

_____

270

8 THINGS YOU SHOULD KNOW ABOUT Sports Biomechanists

1 Sports biomechanists use science to help athletes perform better.

2 Sports biomechanists study the forces that act on the body as it moves.

3 Sports biomechanists use different tools. High-speed cameras and sensors record an athlete's motions. A computer is used to study the data.

4 When seconds count, sports biomechanists can increase an athlete's speed. They can help a runner move faster to win the race.

5 Sports biomechanists show athletes the right way to move so that they don't hurt their bodies.

6 Sports biomechanists study Olympic swimmers using a small pool called a flume.

7 In a wind tunnel, a giant fan moves air over a bicycle and its rider. A sports biomechanist uses this machine to measure how the wind flows past the rider's body.

8 Strong bands called resistance cords are put on an athlete's arms and legs. They can help improve a runner's speed and acceleration.

Be a Sports Biomechanist!

▶ Answer the questions to get to the finish line!

1 What do we call a person trained in a sport? _____

2 Sports biomechanists study the _____ that act on a person's body as it moves.

3 Name a tool that sports biomechanists use. _____

4 What machine is used by swimmers at an Olympic training center? _____

5 Draw a picture of yourself playing your favorite sport.

Think About It

▶ Why would athletes want to see slow-motion videos of themselves playing their sport? _____

4.4.4 Define a problem in the context of motion and transportation and propose a solution to this problem by evaluating, reevaluating and testing the design, gathering evidence about how well the design meets the needs of the problem, and documenting the design so that it can be easily replicated. **Design Process**

Essential Question

What Is an Engineering Design Process?

Engage Your Brain!

Find the answer to the following question in this lesson and record it here.

Why would a car company want a wooden car?

_____

_____

_____

_____

Active Reading

Lesson Vocabulary

List each term. As you learn about each one, make notes in the Interactive Glossary.

_____

_____

_____

Signal Words: Sequence

Signal words show connections between ideas. Words that signal sequence include *now, before, after, first,* and *next.* Active readers remember what they read because they are alert to signal words that identify sequence.

273

What Is ENGINEERING?

From the food we eat and the clothes we wear, to the cars we drive and the phones we talk on, science is at work in our lives every day.

Active Reading As you read the next page, circle the main idea of the text, and put brackets [ ] around each detail sentence.

Electrical engineers use their knowledge of physics to build things like this robot.

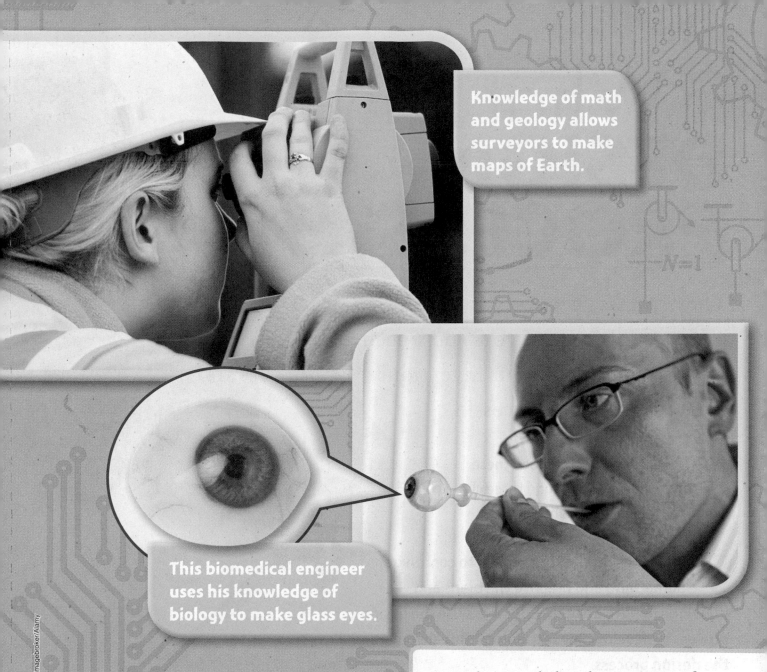

Knowledge of math and geology allows surveyors to make maps of Earth.

This biomedical engineer uses his knowledge of biology to make glass eyes.

Engineering is the use of scientific and mathematical principles to develop something practical.

In other words, engineers use science. Some use biology; others use geology, chemistry, or physics.

Engineers use this knowledge to create something new. It might be a product, a system, or a process for doing things. Whatever it is, it's practical. People use it. Engineers develop things that people use.

▶ In the space below, draw a picture of something you can see around you that was probably designed by an engineer.

What Is the DESIGN PROCESS?

They say that necessity is the mother of invention. But once you find a need, how do you build your invention? That's the design process!

Active Reading As you read these two pages, draw boxes around three clue words that signal a sequence or order.

What is design? **Design** means to conceive something and prepare the plans and drawings for it to be built. Engineers use the design process to develop new technology. But anyone can follow the design process.

From basic to complex, skateboards have changed over time.

It starts with identifying a need or a problem that needs to be solved. Next, brainstorm potential solutions. Don't forget to write down all your ideas. You'll need to refer to them later. Once you have some options, select a solution to try. Usually, engineers test possible solutions using a prototype. A **prototype** is an original or test model on which a real product is based. If the prototype works, then the real product is made. Usually, after testing the prototype, adjustments have to be made, and the prototype has to be tested again. Finally, a finished product is made.

Even something seemingly simple takes a lot of thought, planning, testing, and improvement.

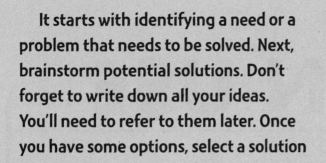

What Do I Need?

Write a problem that could be solved by designing a new product.

_____

_____

_____

_____

_____

277

Design YOU CAN USE

Look around you at all the things you use every day. Do you have ideas about improving them?

Active Reading As you read these two pages, find and underline the meaning of the word *prototype*.

Who Needs It?

The first step in any design process is identifying a need. Is there a chore that could be easier, a tool that could work much better, or a car that could go faster or be safer? Often, the design process begins with the phrase "What if?"

Prototype!

A prototype is a test version of a design. To build a prototype, a person has to have plans. Early sketches give a rough idea. More detailed drawings provide exact measurements for every piece. Keeping good records and drawings helps to make sure that the prototype can be replicated.

This skateboard turns fairly well. But what if it could go around curves even better?

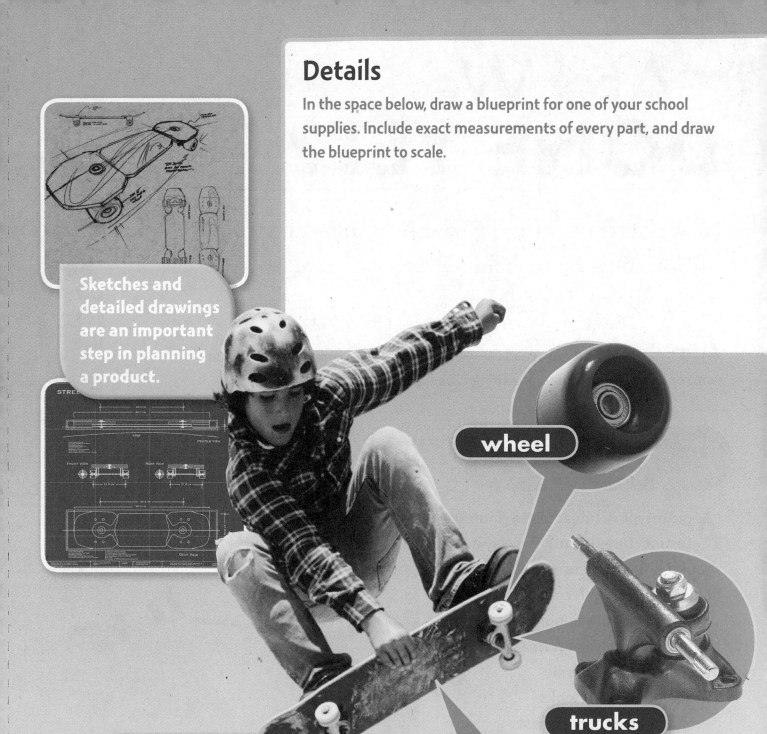

Details

In the space below, draw a blueprint for one of your school supplies. Include exact measurements of every part, and draw the blueprint to scale.

Sketches and detailed drawings are an important step in planning a product.

Every part of a product can become an opportunity for a design change.

wheel

trucks

deck

Are We DONE YET?

Now that the prototype has been built, can the final product be far behind? Yes, it can. But it might not be. It all depends.

Active Reading As you read these two pages, draw a box around the clue word or phrase that signals one thing is being contrasted with another.

Test it!

A prototype is subjected to rigorous testing. Does it work the way it should? Is it easy to use? How does it hold up under harsh conditions?

Even a non-functioning prototype might be shown to hundreds of people, all of whom will comment on how it looks.

It is possible that the first prototype could pass all its tests. Then the product can go into production.

If a prototype works as expected, it will become a finished product.

Keep Improving

But, more often, a prototype is tested in order to find out how the design needs to be changed. Once the test results are collected and analyzed, it's back to the drawing board. The product may need a few tweaks. Or it may need to be completely redesigned.

Sometimes, one prototype leads to ideas for others.

Spin Off!

Imagine a normal bicycle. Now, think of three ways it could be modified to work better in different environments.

_____

_____

_____

_____

New ideas keep the engineering design process constantly moving forward.

When you're done, use the answer key to check and revise your work.

Use information in the summary to complete the graphic organizer.

Summarize

The design process starts with a need or a problem to be solved. The problem must be clearly defined. Next, an engineer brainstorms potential solutions and selects a solution to test. Then, the engineer draws sketches and makes detailed plans and drawings of the product that will be tested. The next step in the design process is to build and test a prototype. The engineer uses the results of these tests to make modifications to the prototype, and tests it again. Finally, a finished product is built.

The design process starts with identifying a need or problem to be solved.

2

Finally, a finished product is built.

1

3

Answer Key: 1. Potential solutions are brainstormed, and a solution to test is selected. **2.** Then, the engineer draws sketches and makes plans and drawings of the product that will be tested. **3.** A prototype is built and tested, and test results are used to modify the prototype for further testing.

Name _____

Word Play

1 Use the clues to help you write the correct word in each row. Tall boxes contain multiple copies of one letter. Some boxes have been filled in for you.

A. To conceive something and prepare plans to build it

B. The use of scientific and mathematical principles to develop something practical

C. A prototype may undergo many rounds of this.

D. Engineers have to be familiar with these principles.

E. The answer to a problem

F. A test version of something

G. The design process can be used to solve this.

H. What comes after sketches, plans, and the prototype?

I. Something that people will use is described as this.

J. Engineers have to be familiar with these principles.

Grid letters given:
- Row A: E, I
- Row B: E, I, G
- Row C: I, G
- Row D: I
- Row E: O, I
- Row F: P, O
- Row G: P, O
- Row H: P, O
- Row I: P, C, L
- Row J: C, L

Apply Concepts

2 Write numbers in the circles to put the pictures in the correct order.

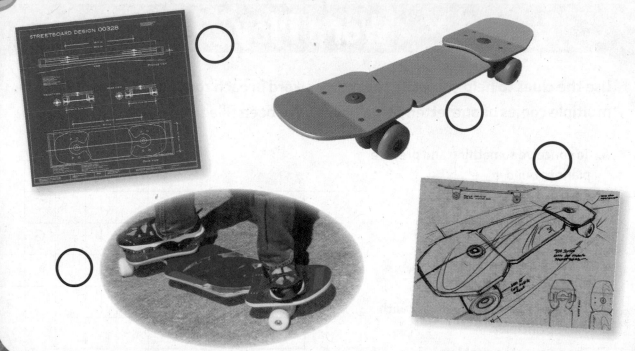

3 How is a prototype different from the finished product?

_____

_____

_____

_____

_____

4 Why is it better to build and test a prototype of a product than to produce tens of thousands of the product and then test it?

_____

_____

_____

5 An engineer who works for a safety apparel company is told, "We want you to design a better helmet for skateboarders." How would you improve these instructions?

_____

_____

_____

_____

6 Which job is more likely to be done by an engineer? Why?

Developing a new material that will be used to make the outer covering of vitamin capsules	Determining how vitamins are absorbed into the bloodstream

_____

_____

_____

_____

_____

_____

_____

7 The engineers at an appliance company have developed a new dishwasher. It looks very different from previous models. The controls look different and work differently. The part of the machine that heats the water has been completely redesigned. Now that the plans are completed, should the company start producing thousands of these dishwashers? Why or why not?

_____

_____

_____

_____

_____

_____

_____

_____

_____

_____

_____

_____

_____

_____

Take It Home! With your family, find a product in your home that needs improving. Imagine you work for the company that makes this product, and brainstorm a new prototype to test.

Name _____

4.4.4 Define a problem in the context of motion and transportation and propose a solution to this problem by evaluating, reevaluating and testing the design, gathering evidence about how well the design meets the needs of the problem, and documenting the design so that it can be easily replicated. **Nature of Science, Design Process**

Essential Question

How Can You Design a Solution to a Problem?

Set a Purpose
What do you think you will learn from this experiment?

_____

_____

_____

Think About the Procedure
How will the equipment you design be similar to safety belts and airbags in a car?

_____

_____

_____

_____

_____

_____

Why is it a good idea to make sure the plastic bag is tightly sealed before you test your prototype?

_____

_____

_____

Record Your Data
In the space below, draw a table to record the materials you used in your prototype and your observations from each test.

Draw Conclusions

What conclusions can you draw as a result of your test observations?

_____

_____

_____

Analyze and Extend

1. Was your design successful? Why or why not?

_____

_____

_____

2. Based on your results, how could you improve your design? Describe and draw the changes you would make to your prototype.

_____

_____

_____

3. Were there any aspects of someone else's design you might incorporate into your design?

_____

_____

_____

4. What is the difference between a successful design and a successful prototype?

_____

_____

_____

_____

5. Think of other questions you would like to ask about forces and transportation.

_____

_____

_____

_____

Multiple Choice

4.4.2

1 An object moves from point A to point B in 2 minutes, at a constant rate.

A   18 meters   B

What is the VELOCITY of the object?

(A) 2 min/m

(B) 9 min/m

(C) 9 m/min

(D) 18 m/min

4.4.1

2 A train moves along rails. What force acts between the rails and the train to SLOW the train's motion?

(A) buoyancy

(B) friction

(C) gravity

(D) thrust

4.4.2

3 The table shows the distances between three points in a park.

Distances in the Park	
Description	Distance (m)
Water fountain to swings	72
Swings to footpath	38
Foot path to snack bar	41

A person walks from the water fountain to the swings, to the footpath, and then to the snack bar in 87 seconds (s). What is the person's AVERAGE SPEED in meters per second (m/s)?

(A) about 0.6 m/s

(B) about 1.2 m/s

(C) about 1.5 m/s

(D) about 1.7 m/s

4.4.3

4 A girl is throwing a ball high into the air and then catching it. What force is responsible for the ball's coming back to the ground?

(A) acceleration

(B) friction

(C) gravity

(D) thrust

4.4.3

5 A soccer ball is rolling across a field. Which force acts OPPOSITE to the direction of the ball's motion?

(A) friction

(B) gravity

(C) lift

(D) weight

4.4.4

6 A class has designed and made model sailboats to learn about how boats move in water. The force of the wind makes the boats move forward. What force should they try to reduce to make the boats move FASTER?

(A) buoyancy

(B) drag

(C) gravity

(D) lift

4.4.4, Design Process

7 A company wants to build a new type of spaceship for transporting astronauts to the moon. What should they do FIRST?

(A) build a model

(B) plan a prototype

(C) test the prototype

(D) evaluate the design

4.4.1

8 A plane is flying through the air. What effect does LIFT have on the plane?

(A) pushes it upward

(B) pushes it forward

(C) pulls it downward

(D) pushes it backward

4.4.2

9 Which of the following has the GREATEST average speed?

(A) a car that travels 180 kilometers in 3 hours

(B) a car that travels 250 kilometers in 5 hours

(C) a car that travels 160 kilometers in 4 hours

(D) a car that travels 140 kilometers in 2 hours

4.4.4, Design Process

10 Some students designed and built two model race cars. They tested their cars using two tracks that were flat and straight. Now, they want to change the track for the blue car and repeat the experiment. Below are the data from their first tests. In what way should they change the track for the blue car so that the factors affecting the tests are the same?

Car	Distance traveled (m)	Time taken (s)	Direction of motion
red	10	5	west
blue	20	20	east

(A) Move the track so the car travels west.

(B) Add another piece of straight track to the end of the track.

(C) Replace one straight piece of track with a curved piece of track.

(D) Put a block at the end of the track to stop the car when it reaches the end.

4.4.1

11 A pitcher throws a ball toward a batter. What effect does GRAVITY have on the ball?

(A) pulls it upward

(B) pushes it forward

(C) pulls it downward

(D) pushes it backward

4.4.1

12 A boy is pulling a box by a rope across the ground, as shown in the figure.

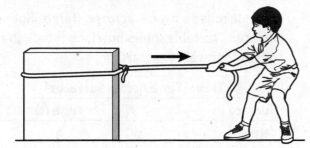

What FORCE is working AGAINST the boy's pulling?

(A) acceleration
(B) friction
(C) gravity
(D) velocity

4.4.4

13 The steps leading into a building are slippery. What change would make the steps SAFER?

(A) decrease lift
(B) decrease drag
(C) increase gravity
(D) increase friction

4.4.1

14 A girl is swinging on a swing. When she gets off, the swing continues to move for a while, but soon it stops. What force causes the swing to STOP?

(A) buoyancy
(B) friction
(C) gravity
(D) thrust

4.4.2

15 A truck is traveling a distance of 320 kilometers. What would the total travel time for the truck have to be in order for its average speed to be close to 55 kilometers per hour?

(A) 6 hours
(B) 7 hours
(C) 8 hours
(D) 9 hours

4.4.1

16 Acceleration is a measure related to motion. What is ACCELERATION?

(A) the rate at which velocity changes
(B) a measure of the speed of something
(C) a unit of distance in the metric system
(D) the energy associated with pushing or pulling

4.4.2

17 A car is traveling at an average speed of 45 kilometers per hour. At this speed, how long will it take the car to travel 225 kilometers?

(A) 5 hours
(B) 6 hours
(C) 7 hours
(D) 8 hours

4.4.3

18 The table shows the distances and times a ball rolls during an investigation. For each trial, the ball starts from rest and a force causes it to move.

Motion of the Ball		
Trial	Time (s)	Distance (m)
1	3	12
2	6	18
3	8	16
4	3	6

Based on the data, during which trial did the GREATEST force cause the ball to move?

(A) Trial 1
(B) Trial 2
(C) Trial 3
(D) Trial 4

4.4.1

19 A skater is sliding on skates across ice. What effect does DRAG have on the skater?

(A) pulls him upward
(B) pushes him forward
(C) pulls him downward
(D) pushes him backward

4.4.1

20 In which example is a force causing an object to ACCELERATE?

(A) a soccer ball sitting on the ground
(B) a rock sitting on a ledge at the top of a mountain
(C) a train moving at constant speed around a curve in a track
(D) a girl riding a bicycle at a constant speed along a straight path

Constructed Response

4.4.1

21 Amanda rolled a toy car across different floor surfaces. The table shows how long it took the toy car to travel 10 meters.

Travel Time Across Surfaces	
Surface	Time (s)
carpet	6
wood floor	3
tile floor	3

Identify the FORCE that changed the speed of the toy car on the different surfaces.

_____

_____

In which DIRECTION did this force act?

_____

_____

What do the data suggest about how the surface affects the speed of a moving object?

_____

_____

_____

_____

4.4.1

22 A plane moves at a constant speed through the air. Identify the four forces acting on the plane and the directions in which they act.

(1) _____

(2) _____

(3) _____

(4) _____

Later, the plane's speed decreases, but its height above the ground does not change. Describe the change in forces that causes the speed to decrease.

_____

_____

_____

4.4.4, Design Process

23 A company builds a simple snow sled out of a rounded piece of plastic. During testing, they find the sled does not slide very fast.

Explain why it is important for the company to test and evaluate the design of the sled.

_____

_____

_____

Describe how the company might change the sled so that the forces on it will make the sled move FASTER.

_____

_____

_____

Extended Response

4.4.4, Design Process

24 An engineer is producing a new type of roller coaster for an amusement park. The first step is to design the roller coaster.

Why is it important to keep good notes during the design process?

_____

_____

_____

Identify TWO forces that act on the roller coaster, and explain how they affect its motion.

_____

_____

_____

_____

_____

Why should the engineer build a prototype of the roller coaster?

_____

_____

_____

Describe a part of the design process the engineer should do AFTER testing the prototype.

_____

_____

_____

_____

4.4.4

25 The diagram below shows two heavy balls being held in position with four ropes.

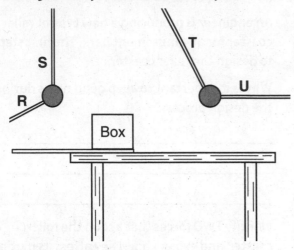

Is gravity acting on the box? Explain how you know.

_____

_____

_____

_____

Cutting one of the ropes will cause the box to move in a direction OPPOSITE to a ball's motion. Which rope is this? Describe the forces and the motion.

_____

_____

_____

_____

Cutting one of the ropes will cause the box to move in the SAME DIRECTION as the ball's motion. Which rope is this? Describe the forces and the motion.

_____

_____

_____

_____

Explain how you can cut one of the ropes and cause a ball to move WITHOUT moving the box.

_____

_____

_____

_____

Interactive Glossary

As you learn about each term, add notes, drawings, or sentences in the extra space. This will help you remember what the terms mean. Here are some examples.

fungi [FUHN•jee] A kingdom of organisms, with a nucleus, that get nutrients by decomposing other organisms.

A mushroom is an example of fungi.

physical change [FIHZ•ih•kuhl CHAYNJ] Change in the size, shape, or state of matter with no new substance being formed.

When I cut paper in half, that's a physical change.

Glossary Pronunciation Key

With every glossary term, there is also a phonetic respelling. A phonetic respelling writes the word the way it sounds, which can help you pronounce new or unfamiliar words. Use this key to help you understand the respellings.

Sound	As in	Phonetic Respelling	Sound	As in	Phonetic Respelling
a	bat	(BAT)	oh	over	(OH•ver)
ah	lock	(LAHK)	oo	pool	(POOL)
air	rare	(RAIR)	ow	out	(OWT)
ar	argue	(AR•gyoo)	oy	foil	(FOYL)
aw	law	(LAW)	s	cell	(SEL)
ay	face	(FAYS)		sit	(SIT)
ch	chapel	(CHAP•uhl)	sh	sheep	(SHEEP)
e	test	(TEST)	th	that	(THAT)
	metric	(MEH•trik)		thin	(THIN)
ee	eat	(EET)	u	pull	(PUL)
	feet	(FEET)	uh	medal	(MED•uhl)
	ski	(SKEE)		talent	(TAL•uhnt)
er	paper	(PAY•per)		pencil	(PEN•suhl)
	fern	(FERN)		onion	(UHN•yuhn)
eye	idea	(eye•DEE•uh)		playful	(PLAY•fuhl)
i	bit	(BIT)		dull	(DUHL)
ing	going	(GOH•ing)	y	yes	(YES)
k	card	(KARD)		ripe	(RYP)
	kite	(KYT)	z	bags	(BAGZ)
ngk	bank	(BANGK)	zh	treasure	(TREZH•er)

Interactive Glossary

A

acceleration [ak•sel•er•AY•shuhn] Any change in the speed or direction of an object's motion (p. 250)

adaptation [ad•uhp•TAY•shuhn] A trait or characteristic that helps an organism survive (p. 210)

B

buoyant force [boy·uhnt FAWRS] The upward force exerted on an object by water (p. 257)

C

circuit [SER•kuht] A path along which electric charges can flow (p. 82)

computer model [kuhm•PYOO•ter MOD•l] A computer program that models an event or object (p. 49)

conduction [kuhn•DUK•shuhn] The movement of heat between two materials that are touching (p. 114)

D

conductor [kuhn•DUK•ter] Materials that let heat or electrical charges travel through them easily (p. 80)

data [DEY•tuh] Individual facts, statistics, and items of information (p. 37)

conservation [kahn•ser•VAY•shuhn] The preserving and protecting of a resource (pp. 172, 229)

deposition [dep•uh•ZISH•uhn] The dropping or settling of eroded materials (p. 136)

convection [kuhn•VEK•shuhn] The movement of heat in liquids and gases from a warmer area to a cooler area (p.115)

design [dih·ZYN] To prepare the plans and drawings for something to be built (p. 276)

displace [dis·PLEYS] To move a substance or object away from its original position (p. 256)

electric current [ee•LEK•trik KER•uhnt] The flow of electric charges along a path (p. 72)

drag [DRAG] A slowing force that acts on an object moving through liquid or air; drag from the air slows an airplane (p. 255)

electric motor [ee•LEK•trik MOHT•er] A device that changes electrical energy into mechanical energy (p. 98)

E

earthquake [ERTH·kwayk] A shaking of Earth's surface that can cause land to rise and fall (p. 152)

electromagnet [ee•lek•troh•MAG•nit] A temporary magnet caused by an electric current (p. 101)

engineering [en•juh•NIR•ing] The application of science to practical uses such as the design of structures, machines, and systems (p. 275)

evidence [EV•uh•duhns] Information collected during a scientific investigation (p. 12)

environment [en•VY•ruhn•muhnt] All the living and nonliving things that surround and affect an organism (p. 208)

extinction [ek•STINGK•shuhn] The death of all the organisms of a certain kind of living thing (p. 226)

F

erosion [uh•ROH•zhuhn] The process of moving sediment from one place to another (p. 136)

force [FAWRS] A push or a pull of any kind (p. 250)

fossil fuel [FAHS•uhl FYOO•uhl] Fuel formed from the remains of once living things. Coal, oil, and natural gas are fossil fuels.(p. 170)

glacier [GLAY•shur] A huge body of ice and snow that moves over land (p. 139, 142)

friction [FRIK•shuhn] A force that acts between two touching objects and that opposes motion (p. 112, 252)

gravity [GRAV•ih•tee]The force of attraction between objects, such as the attraction between Earth and objects on it (p. 252)

G

generator [GRAV•ih•tee] A device that makes an electric current by converting kinetic energy to electrical energy (p. 103)

H

heat [HEET] The energy that moves between objects of different temperatures (p. 110)

heredity [huh•RED•ih•tee] The process by which traits are passed from parents to offspring (p. 193)

instinct [IN•stinkt] An inherited behavior of an animal that helps it meet its needs (p. 200)

hypothesis [hy•PAHTH•uh•sis] A possible explanation or answer to a question; a testable statement (p. 9)

insulator [IN•suh•layt•er] A material that does not let heat or electrical charges move through it easily (p. 80)

inference [IN•fer•uhns] An untested conclusion based on your observations (p. 19)

investigation [in•ves•tuh•GAY•shuhn] A procedure carried out to gather data about an object or event (p. 7)

L

landslide [LAND•slyd] A form of erosion when gravity makes soil, mud, and rocks move quickly down a slope. Landslides can happen suddenly especially after heavy rains or earthquakes (p. 156)

learned behavior [LERND bee•HAYV•yer] A behavior that an animal develops as a result of experience or by observing other animals (p. 202)

lift [LIFT] An upward force acting on an object (p. 258)

M

microscope [MY•kruh•skohp] A tool that makes an object look several times bigger than it is (p. 33)

model [MOD•l] A mental or physical representation of a process or object (p. 47)

motion [MOH•shuhn] A change of position of an object (p. 245)

N

nonrenewable resource
[nahn•rih•NOO•uh•buhl REE•sawrs] A resource that, once used, cannot be replaced in a reasonable amount of time (p. 169)

O

observation [ahb•zuhr•VAY•shuhn] Information that you gather with your senses (p. 7)

P

pan balance [PAN BAL•uhns] A tool that measures mass (p. 34)

parallel circuit [PAIR•uh•lel SER•kit] An electric circuit that has more than one path for the electric charges to follow (p. 85)

pollution [puh•LOO•shuhn] Any harmful substance in the environment (p. 168, 223)

Interactive Glossary

position [puh•ZISH•uhn] The location of an object in relation to a nearby object or place (p. 245)

recycle [ree•SY•kuhl] To use the materials in old things to make new things (p. 175)

prototype [PROH•tuh•typ] The original or model on which something is based (p. 277)

renewable resource [rih•NOO•uh•buhl REE•sawrs] A resource that can be replaced within a reasonable amount of time (p. 169)

R

radiation [ray•dee•AY•shuhn] The movement of heat without matter to carry it (p. 117)

resource [REE•sawrs] Any material that can be used to satisfy a need (p. 168)

R10

S

science [SY•uhns] The study of the natural world (p. 5)

series circuit [SIR•eez SER•kit] An electric circuit in which the electrical charges have only one path to follow (p. 85)

scientist [SY•uhn•tist] A person who asks questions about the natural world (p. 5)

speed [SPEED] The measure of an object's change in position during a certain amount of time (p. 248)

sediment [SED•uh•ment] Small pieces of rock, sand, and silt carried by water (p. 137)

spring scale [SPRING SKAYL] A tool that measures forces, such as weight (p. 34)

Interactive Glossary

static electricity [STAT•ik ee•lek•TRIS•uh•tee] The buildup of electric charges on an object (p. 69)

T

three-dimensional model [THREE-di•MEN•shuh•nuhl MOD•l] A model that has the dimension of depth as well as width and height (p. 49)

two-dimensional model [TOO-di•MEN•shuh•nuhl MOD•l] A model that has the dimensions of width and height only (p. 47)

V

velocity [vuh•LAHS•uh•tee] The speed of an object in a particular direction (p. 248)

volcano [vahl•KAY•noh] A place where hot gases, smoke, and melted rock come out of the ground onto Earth's surface (p. 155)

W

weathering [WETH•er•ing] The breaking down of rocks on Earth's surface into smaller pieces (p. 134)

Index

Index

order, 22, 41, 93, 247, 276, 284

plan investigation, 21

predict, 20, 25, 33, 219

record data, 23, 26, 36–37, 40, 43, 93, 123, 149, 165, 181, 219, 267, 269, 287

sequence, 77, 95–96, 160, 178, 273, 276

use numbers, 22, 26

use time/space relationships, 22–23, 25

use variables, 20, 25

using models, 50, 55–56

Insects, 225

ant, 32

bee, 201

butterfly, 36

fly, 250–251

honeybee, 38–39

ladybug, 29

leaf cutter ant, 33

wasp, 232

Instinct, 200-201, 204, 205, 206

animals, 200

bee, 201

fish, 201

human, 200

squirrel, 201

vs. learned behavior, 201, 206

Insulator, 80–81, 88, 90, 123–124. *See also* **Conductor**

International Space Station, 261

Interpret data, 227

Investigation, 2, 7–8, 15, 21, 24, 26, 29, 93

ISTEP+ Practice, 57–62, 125–130, 183–188, 235–240, 289–294

Kinetic energy, 103. *See also* **Energy**

Landform, 145

delta, 137

dunes, 138

arch, 133, 141, 147

Landslide, 140, 156, 159, 161–162

compare and contrast, 157

Lava, 154–155, 159–160

Learned behavior, 202-203, 204, 205, 206

chimpanzee, 203

parrot, 201

racehorse, 201

vs. instinct, 201, 206

Life scientist, 5

Lift, 258

Light energy, 89–90, 99, 105. *See also* **Energy**

Lightning, 71, 74

Living things. *See also* **Animals; Plants**

adaptation, 210–211

bat, 190

and change, 198–199

characteristics of, 190

cause weathering, 134–135

environment, 197, 207–209

heredity, 193

human impact, 221–229

traits, 194

Maathai, Wangari, 233

Magma, 155, 159–160

Magnifying box, 33, 41. *See also* **Science tools**

Main Idea and Details, 3, 12, 17, 29, 36, 52, 65–66, 68, 70, 72, 105, 114, 191, 194, 196, 198, 204, 243, 260, 274

Make a model, 47–48

Mammals, 23

arctic hare, 213

baby horse, 200

bat, 189–190

calf, 200

chimpanzee, 203

cow, 265

giraffe, 193

jackrabbit, 212–213

orangutan, 233

polar bear, 226

prairie dog, 210–211

racehorse, 201

rabbit, 248–249

sloth, 211

spider monkey, 218

squirrel, 201, 205, 225

Tasmanian wolf, 227

whale, 23

zebra, 191

Marine biologist, 21–22

Mars, 48

surface of, 10

Mathematics Skills. *See* **Do the Math!**

Measure, 17, 22, 25–26, 34–35, 42–44, 55–56, 140, 242, 248, 255, 262, 279

Measurement tools. *See* **Science tools**

Mechanical energy, 96, 98–99, 102, 105–106. *See also* **Energy**

Mental model, 53. *See also* **Model**

Metal, 123–124

Meteorologist, 50

Microscope, 33, 41–42. *See also* **Science tools**

Model. *See also* **Make a model**

computer, 49–50, 52–53

mental, 53

rock, 140

to save lives, 50–51

scale, 49, 53

Index